TYPE

PERFECT TYPEFACE COMBINATIONS
Tony Seddon

Contents

On this page: HTF Didot Light from Hoefler & Co.

The Principles

The Tricks

Introduction

On this page: The Carpenter Regular from Fenotype

Choosing a typeface is a bit like deciding what music to listen to. You run through your collection of CDs or MP3 downloads, something catches your eye, and you press 'play'. You might have chosen the album or track because you're in a contemplative mood, or you're driving a fast car or you're sitting down to eat dinner with your friends. Typefaces are chosen for specific reasons too: because they're legible, because they're indicative of a particular period in time or because they match the mood of the text.

Continuing with the music analogy, most people like at least two or three musical styles; maybe some Bluegrass or Art Punk with a few show tunes thrown in for good measure. If you set up a playlist on your phone, you'll think about the running order, which probably means not adding a heavy-metal track in the middle of the *The Magic Flute*. Once again, a similar idea applies when choosing typefaces; if you're picking two or three to use in combination, it's important to think about how they relate to one another, and to the subject matter of the text. Even if you're a fan of both Motörhead and Mozart, the examples above are no more harmonious than if Fette Fraktur (page 153) were paired with SangBleu (page 216).

So to the big question: what are the best typeface combinations? Unfortunately, there's no straight answer. There are plenty of established principles and tricks that can help you make a decision and many of them are explained in this book, but putting together typefaces in perfect combination is ultimately as subjective as it is scientific, as personal as it is informed and as debated as it is agreed upon. There are 149 suggested Type Team combinations in this book, and ultimately they're exactly that – *suggestions*. Some of them may be perfect for your next project but you may look at others and think, 'Why did he put that with that? I would never combine those typefaces', and that would be fair enough. I also realise that you'll not have all of these fonts in your own collections – neither would I if it weren't for the generosity of the type foundries and individual designers who provided their typefaces for use in this book – but there's a good chance that you'll have something similar that you can sub in for one of my suggestions, perhaps Clarendon instead of Eames Century Modern, or New Century Schoolbook instead of Farnham.

Either way, I hope that this book provides you with the information and the inspiration required to make the best choices you can when bringing typefaces together, and that you gain as much from reading it as I did while writing and designing it.

Classification

There have been several attempts during the last hundred years or so to come up with a definitive system for typeface classification, but they've all been flawed in one way or another. The Vox-ATypI system, devised by the French historian Maximilien Vox in 1954 and adopted by the Association Typographique Internationale in 1967, has come as close as any to getting it right but it's now considered inadequate. Many innovative typefaces created in the last thirty years have been designed to address the challenge of being able to function well across a wide range of print and screen environments, but in turn this means they're difficult to categorise by association with a recognised historical style. It's now perfectly legitimate to consider a face to be a Humanist Transitional or a Neo-Grotesque Geometric. However, Vox-ATypI is still a useful place to start (with an open-minded approach) and the categories listed to the right are based around the system with one or two additional categories, which I hope will help you to recognise potential pairing possibilities between different faces with similar characteristics.

The examples shown beneath each classification are of course not always *actual* typefaces from the time period indicated but rather digital revivals of the styles.

On this page: Farnham Display Light from The Font Bureau

Ancient pre-fifteenth century; includes Blackletter (or Fraktur) and Incised (or Antique).
Examples: Goudy Medieval 𝕱𝖊𝖙𝖙𝖊 𝕱𝖗𝖆𝖐𝖙𝖚𝖗

Humanist also called Venetian; serifs from the mid-fifteenth century onwards. Sans serifs with calligraphic roots are now also referred to as Humanist.
Examples: Adobe Jenson Requiem

Old Style also called Garalde; serifs from the late fifteenth century onwards.
Examples: Adobe Caslon Mercury

Transitional serifs from the mid-eighteenth century onwards; includes Scotch Roman.
Examples: Farnham Le Monde Livre

Modern also called Didone; serifs from the late eighteenth century onwards. Very bold Moderns are known as Fat Face.
Examples: Bodoni Abril

Slab also known as Square Serif; from the early nineteenth century onwards. Traditionally split into Clarendons (bracketed serifs) and Egyptians (unbracketed serifs), they are now more commonly referred to as either Grotesque Slabs, Geometric Slabs or Humanist Slabs.
Examples: Eames Century Modern Vitesse

Sans serif from the early nineteenth but more prolific from the twentieth century onwards. Sub classifications include Grotesque, Neo-Grotesque, Gothic, Square, Geometric, Humanist and Neo-Humanist.
Examples: FS Emeric Colfax

Display from the nineteenth century onwards; faces that were designed purely for use at large point sizes and are unsuitable for smaller text setting.
Examples: Acropolis Giza

Script from the late eighteenth century onwards; split into Formal, Casual and Calligraphic.
Examples: Bickham Script Liza Text

Glyphic from the twentieth century onwards.
Examples: Albertus Modesto

Contemporary from the later twentieth century onwards; faces that feature innovative designs that are amalgams of other classifications and therefore defy specific classification. These are almost exclusively faces designed after the introduction of PostScript in 1982.
Examples: FS Olivia Doko

Type Teams

On this page: Neutraface Slab Display Bold from House Industries

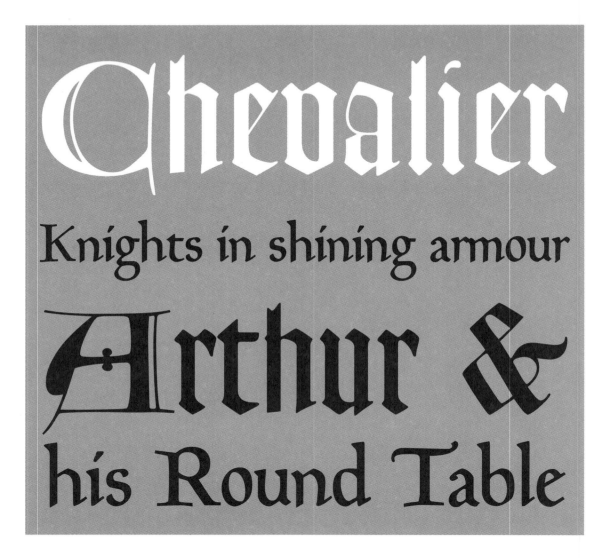

In terms of Western typographic history, typeface design didn't exist prior to the introduction of movable type in the mid-fifteenth century. Handwritten letterforms provided the natural models for the earliest typeface designs, known as Gothic or Blackletter, and the relatively contemporary Goudy Medieval and Goudy Lombardic Capitals, designed by Frederic Goudy in 1915 and 1928 respectively, are good choices when a medieval flavour is required.

On this page

Goudy Lombardic Capitals

Goudy Medieval

Middle Ages
Carolingian
feudalism
Johannes Gutenberg's 42-line Bible

Cabazon, designed by Jim Parkinson in 2005, is a textura-style Blackletter revival that succeeds where others fail because it's relatively free of the fussy details that create legibility issues with other Blackletter faces. Combine it with 2012's Eskapade Fraktur from TypeTogether for a modern take on the medieval theme, and for small text such as captions or footnotes use Hoefler & Co.'s Gothic-style sans serif Whitney with its distinctive angled terminals.

On this page

Cabazon

Eskapade Fraktur

Whitney

FLORENCE

Michelangelo

David

Lorenzo de'Medici

The Renaissance began in Italy in the fourteenth century and spread throughout Europe with the propagation of ideas gaining pace on the introduction of movable type in the mid-fifteenth century. Hoefler & Co.'s Requiem was inspired by illustrations from a sixteenth-century writing manual and is a fine realisation of a Humanist style serif. Sans serif typefaces didn't exist during this period but Verlag will work if a contemporary twist is appropriate.

On this page

Requiem Display
Requiem Text
Verlag

REFORM
A.D. 1722
Brackets
English Foundry

Caslon first appeared in the eighteenth century and has remained in popular use ever since. Many versions have made it to the digital platform for use at smaller point sizes but they don't work well when set larger for headlines. However, Big Caslon from Carter & Cone successfully revives the Caslon foundry's display cuts and pairs well with Adobe Caslon, arguably the most even-handed digital revival of the original cut, when it's used for text setting.

On this page
Big Caslon
Adobe Caslon

Victorian VOGUE

Although this book offers suggestions for which typefaces work well together depending on the nature of the message you wish to broadcast, please don't be tempted to simply stop short at our suggestions. This will limit the potentially endless options open to you; all good typefaces can work under several different guises, either alone or in combination with others.

For example, a Humanist serif like Jenson is perfect for conjuring a sense of history or an air of scholarly contemplation, but it works equally well for any text that needs to feel richly indulgent thanks to its organic form, a typical feature of typefaces in this classification. As another example, the wonderfully forthright Grotesque

Slab **Giza** is the very epitome of Victorian-era playbill typesetting, but its playful curves combined with the current resurgence of popularity for slabs in general mean it also looks perfectly at home on the cover of a style magazine.

There are of course some typefaces that are intended for one job alone and carry hefty clues in their names. These are often Display faces that are variously tagged as 'Novelty' or 'Ornamental' and are frequently marked down as visually inferior, but they do have a role to play all the same. For example, **Countdown** (that's Countdown!), designed by Colin Brignall for dry transfer company Letraset in 1965, screams 'retro technology' but its role has moved on to being a typeface that can look great on a flyer for a retro club night, demonstrating how typefaces with limited scope can adapt to new or unexpected applications.

Italia
GLORIFICATION
of our cultural heroes
Machiavelli

FF Clifford, released by FontFont in 1999, combines both Humanist and Transitional serif characteristics and is supplied in three separate optical sizes: 6, 9 and 18. This attention to detail helps recreate the feel of a highly readable classic metal typeface, perfect for evoking a period atmosphere. The Humanist serif Centaur MT is a little more hard-edged due to its inscriptional origins and works best as a headline when combined with FF Clifford.

On this page

Centaur MT
FF Clifford

Claude Garamont

Plantin-Moretus Museum

Paraphrasis in Elegantiarum Libros Laurentii Vallae

Text with unsurpassed legibility

The enormously popular Old Style serif Garamond has suffered during its transition from metal to digital type with some unsympathetic interpretations released over the years but Adobe's Garamond Premier, released in 2005, addresses many of those issues. Most importantly, there are now separate subfamilies drawn in specific optical sizes for use as display, text and caption setting, meaning the original character of the face is much restored.

On this page

Garamond Premier Display

Garamond Premier

Garamond Premier Caption

PARADISE LOST
THE AUTHOR
JOHN MILTON

OF MANS FIRST DISOBEDIENCE,
AND THE FRUIT
OF THAT FORBIDDEN TREE,
WHOSE MORTAL TAST
BROUGHT DEATH INTO THE
WORLD, AND ALL OUR WOE,
With loss of Eden, till one greater Man
Restore us, and regain the blissful Seat,
Sing Heav'nly Muse, that on the secret top
Of Oreb, or of Sinai, didst inspire
That Shepherd, who first taught the chosen Seed,
In the Beginning how the Heav'ns and Earth
Rose out of Chaos: Or if Sion Hill
Delight thee more, and Siloa's Brook that flow'd
Fast by the Oracle of God; I thence
Invoke thy aid to my adventrous Song,
That with no middle flight intends to soar
Above th' Aonian Mount, while it pursues
Things unattempted yet in Prose or Rhime.
And chiefly Thou O Spirit, that dost prefer
Before all Temples th' upright heart and pure,
16

Client	The Doves Press
Studio/Designer	T. J. Cobden-Sanderson,
	Emery Walker, Edward Johnston
Principal typefaces	The Doves Type

The Doves Press was a private press established in 1900 in Hammersmith, London, by T. J. Cobden-Sanderson and Emery Walker. All of its publications were set using the same typeface, The Doves Type, which was in turn based on Nicolas Jenson's 1470s Humanist serif. Calligraphic additions were printed using woodblocks created from letterforms drawn by Edward Johnston.

Principle #1 | **Stress**

By definition, *stress* means emphasis or tension. In typographic terms stress indicates the angle of transition from the thickest to the thinnest points in a glyph's stroke. Typographic stress is generally measured along either a near vertical or vertical axis, although some typefaces display horizontal stress characteristics. The latter are also referred to as reversed stress and usually take the form of heavily stylised display faces.

So why do so many typefaces feature a variable stroke width? The answer can be found by looking at the earliest Roman typefaces designed during the fifteenth and sixteenth centuries – Humanist and Old Style serifs – which were based on earlier handwritten letterforms. A prime example is Nicolas Jenson's work from 1470; the handwritten characteristics of the Humanist (or Venetian) glyphs dating from this period produce a moderately variable stroke width and a backwards- or left-leaning angle of stress. The natural angle of a quill or broad-nib pen when held by a right-handed person gives us this backwards-leaning trait.

In contrast, Modern serifs, which began to appear in the late eighteenth century, are based on characters written with a pointed nib. The stroke width increases as the pressure on the nib is increased, causing the nib's tines to move apart. Thicker strokes can only be created by a downwards movement of the pen, otherwise the nib's tines tend to dig into the paper's surface, and it's this that gives Moderns their characteristically vertical stress. Typefaces with little or no stroke contrast (i.e. no visible thinning of the strokes) are also deemed to be vertically stressed.

Circular characters such as the uppercase and lowercase 'O', the uppercase 'Q' and lowercase 'e' are useful glyphs to examine when determining the angle of stress, or stroke axis. To measure the angle, identify the thinnest points of a circular stroke at the highest and lowest points of a glyph and run a line between them. The angle of this line is the angle of stress. When combining typefaces, stress angles can be used either to harmonise, or to create a visual juxtaposition between faces used in a typographic hierarchy.

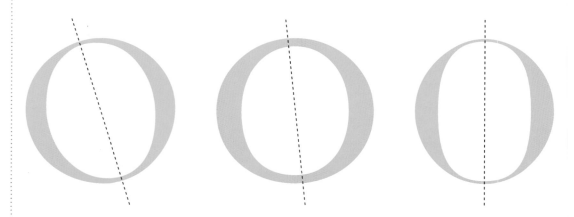

The angle of stress becomes gradually more vertical when moving from Humanist serifs, through Transitional serifs, to Moderns. The typefaces shown here are Adobe Jenson, Baskerville Original and Didot.

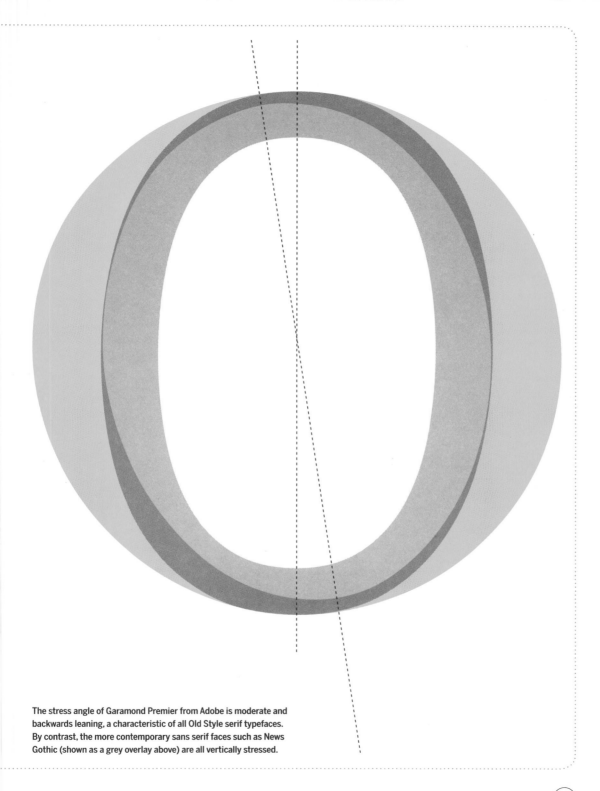

The stress angle of Garamond Premier from Adobe is moderate and backwards leaning, a characteristic of all Old Style serif typefaces. By contrast, the more contemporary sans serif faces such as News Gothic (shown as a grey overlay above) are all vertically stressed.

FINELY CRAFTED SERIF

Ben Franklin

1757

Transitional agreement

Like Garamond, Transitional typeface Baskerville, first released in the 1750s, has suffered during its conversion from metal to digital type. However, Storm's Baskerville Original restores much of the character displayed in the metal cuts of the typeface by once again introducing different optical sizes for large and small setting. Try it alongside FF Yoga Sans if a contrasting sans serif is needed for smaller captions without affecting the historical mood.

On this page

Baskerville Original
FF Yoga Sans

Riesling

Repatriation

1795

The shape of things to come…

Fry's Baskerville was recut for the Fry Typefoundry in the late 1700s to address the perceived shortcomings of the existing cuts of Baskerville when used as a display face, and the finer detailing has long been regarded as a successful interpretation that carried over well when converted to a digital typeface. It pairs nicely with the high contrast and sharp detail of ITC New Baskerville, and the traditional feel of Gill Sans works well if a contrasting sans serif is required.

On this page

Fry's Baskerville
ITC New Baskerville
Gill Sans

Ragazzo

Kaleidoscope

GOLDEN BROWN

The latest bulletin

Despite its seventeenth-century roots, OurType's Arnhem is a thoroughly modern Transitional serif that was designed specifically for use as dense newspaper setting yet manages to retain its historical character. Readability is enhanced by the large x-height, which also allows successful pairing with a broad range of sans serif faces, and the extensive range of optically sized weights provides an enormous amount of practical flexibility within the extended family.

On this page

Arnhem Fine
Arnhem Display
Arnhem Blond
Benton Sans

Skye

Referendum Time

The highs and lows

A relevant political footnote

Chronicle from Hoefler & Co. is another example of a contemporary and beautiful Transitional style typeface designed for use with dense running text printed on uncompromising low-grade newsprint. Strong Scotch Roman characteristics provide elements of approachability and warmth, and it's supplied in four 'grades' designed specifically to get the best out of differing print environments. The straightforward character of Trade Gothic provides a useful partner.

On this page

Chronicle Display
Chronicle Text
Trade Gothic

Emigre's Mrs Eaves is a modern reimagining of Baskerville and is named after John Baskerville's housekeeper and wife. It features a distinctively small x-height, which can create some pairing issues, so it's often used as a one-off signature typeface, but it works very well with classic Formal scripts, which can themselves be difficult to combine successfully with other faces. Bickham Script is one of the best available today and rarely fails to achieve its elegant goals.

On this page

Mrs Eaves

Bickham Script

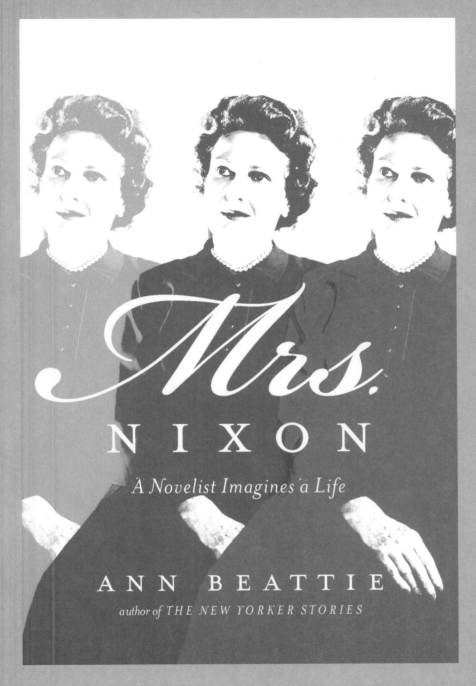

Client	Scribner
Studio/Designer	Jason Heuer, Rex Bonomelli
Web	www.jasonheuer.com
Principal typefaces	Bickham Script, Mrs Eaves

Author Ann Beattie's reconstruction of the life of the only modern-era First Lady to have never written a memoir. The combination of Transitional serif Mrs Eaves and Formal script Bickham Script creates a fresh but formal feel for the cover.

BYRON

Regency London

She walks in beauty

Childe Harold's Pilgrimage

Notorious

Romanticism peaked during the first half of the nineteenth century, coinciding with the surge in popularity for Modern serifs or Didones. HTF Didot is a contemporary Didone designed by Hoefler & Co. in 1991 for the redesign of *Harper's Bazaar* magazine. The full family contains no less than seven optical sizes to allow the setting of everything from a caption to a full-size headline. Pair it with Geometric sans Brandon Grotesque to heighten the sense of romanticism.

On this page

HTF Didot
Brandon Grotesque
Brandon Text

Reginal

Classical form

Gothic Novel

The Legend of Sleepy Hollow

Bauer Bodoni is arguably the archetypal modern serif face and is close in character to the original cut, but it's not much use for small setting because the unbracketed hairline serifs disappear. There are no extra optical sizes to select within this family so it's best used for elegant headlines. Pair it with Font Bureau's Griffith Gothic, which features a subtle thinning at the joints but manages to hold its legibility well when set at smaller point sizes.

On this page

Bauer Bodoni
Griffith Gothic

Trick #2 | Let big personalities have their say

Hey

If you've ever been to a party and been cornered in the kitchen by an overbearing guest, you'll understand this analogy between loud people and loud typefaces. Now, there's nothing wrong with loud people per se; they can be great fun, the life and soul of the party, but you may not want to spend the whole evening with them if you're not equally as loud as they are.

It can be the same with typeface combinations cohabiting a layout. You may choose a Grotesque slab with a massive personality such as **Farao Black** for your headlines and it'll certainly look great with its heavy ball terminals and eccentric curves, but use it wisely. Too much typographic personality concentrated in one space can be overpowering, and the sense of a balanced layout can be lost. The trick is to give the typefaces with a large presence their platform, but at the same time make sure there are other faces present that can offer a quieter opinion to offset that of the big guy at the other end of the room, like *SangBleu*. If you need to set a lot of headings throughout a layout, for example, of a book or magazine, choose a quieter, complementary typeface (perhaps another weight of the same face, the big guy's slighter sibling) to set some of the less important headings and achieve the right balance throughout.

Would anyone like a canapé?

Sturm und Drang

Revolution

Heidelberg

Cornucopia

Der Sandmann

Walbaum was first cut in the early 1800s in Weimar, Germany, and takes its inspiration directly from the likes of Bodoni and Didot. It is unmistakably a Modern serif but it has a few little quirks that provide a more down-to-earth character, with Old Style features in the lowercase glyphs. Pair it with the Humanist slab PMN Caecilia, which also displays characteristics reminiscent of an Old Style book face.

On this page

Walbaum
PMN Caecilia

Zeitgeist

PASSION PLAY

Arch Seductress

Double Cross

In the words of the designer, Neil Summerour of Positype, Lust is 'an indulgent attempt to infuse wanton sensuality in a typeface'. The racily named Lust family incorporates elements of Didone with Scotch Roman and a smattering of Transitional serif, creating a Modern serif that is truly sensual. It's an out-and-out display face of course, so pairing it with a face like Archer that can provide options for smaller setting without spoiling the effect is essential.

On this page

Lust Slim Display

Lust Slim

Archer

Lust Didone

C JOY FILMS PRESENTS "GRACE" A DOLGER FILMS PRODUCTION ANNIKA MARKS, SHARON LAWRENCE, CHASE MOWEN, LIAM SPRINGTHORPE AND CYNTHIA JOY COGGINS CASTING DIRECTOR JUDY HENDERSON C.S.A. COSTUME DESIGNER BEVERLY SAFIER PRODUCTION DESIGNER DARA WISHINGRAD LINE PRODUCER MARK CRANISKY ORIGINAL SCORE COMPOSED BY GARETH PROSSER EDITOR DAVID DEAN DIRECTOR OF PHOTOGRAPHY LUKE GEISSBÜHLER STORY BY C JOY COGGINS SCREENPLAY BY HEATH JONES EXECUTIVE PRODUCER CYNTHIA JOY COGGINS PRODUCED BY SYLVIA CAMINER DIRECTED BY HEATH JONES

gracethemovie.us / facebook: Grace. / twitter: @thegracemovie

Client	Syliva Caminer and Cynthia Joy Goggins/C Joy Films
Studio/Designer	Lure Design/Jeff Matz
Web	www.luredesigninc.com
Principal typefaces	Didot Regular, Triple Condensed Light, Gotham

The graceful form of Didot is used here to express the transformation of the movie's main character from alcoholic addiction to redemption, whilst Triple Condensed takes care of the large amount of information at the poster's base.

VARIETY

Dan Leno

AN ALL STAR CAST

Full Steam Ahead!

from start to finish

The Victorian era conveys a distinct typographic heritage linked indelibly to heavy 'Egyptian' Slab serifs and Clarendons. Several successful digital revivals capture the essence of this era; Ziggurat by Hoefler & Co. is the cornerstone of *The Proteus Project*, a collection of four nineteenth-century headline styles. It pairs well with their Knockout family of condensed sans serifs, and with Old Style serif MVB Verdigris from MVB Fonts.

On this page

Ziggurat

MVB Verdigris

Knockout

My dearest wife

The travails of travel

Reigning regally

your loving husband

Calligraphic scripts that work are difficult to come by, but Aquiline Two makes a pretty good stab at recreating antique-style handwriting. These faces always work better at smaller sizes because they're designed to replicate handwriting, but the odd illustrative headline can look fine. Pair it with classic Transitional face Baskerville Original from Storm, or Old Style serif Adobe Caslon, for an authentic Victorian feeling.

On this page

Aquiline Two
Baskerville Original
Adobe Caslon

STOP PRESS

The crisis deepens

From our *foreign* correspondent

Hold the front page!

Bureau Grot from Font Bureau is a terrific revival of the classic nineteenth-century sans serif. It dates from 1989 and was drawn using original specimens from the Stephenson Blake foundry in Sheffield. The family has expanded to twelve styles over the years and captures the character of Victorian-era typography perfectly. Scotch Roman, a class of typeface that falls within the Transitional classification, completes the antique semblance.

On this page

Bureau Grot

Scotch Roman MT

WANTED!
Dead or Alive
BILLY THE KID
Jack the Ripper
Reward

Clarendon is the archetypal English slab serif typeface, designed originally by Robert Besley in 1845 for the Fann Street Foundry in the City of London. Its popularity during the Victorian era knew no bounds and other foundries eagerly copied and distributed the design, notably in America. The letterforms are so strong that a face which also has considerable character should be paired with Clarendon. Geometric sans Brown from Lineto will hold its own.

On this page
Clarendon
Brown

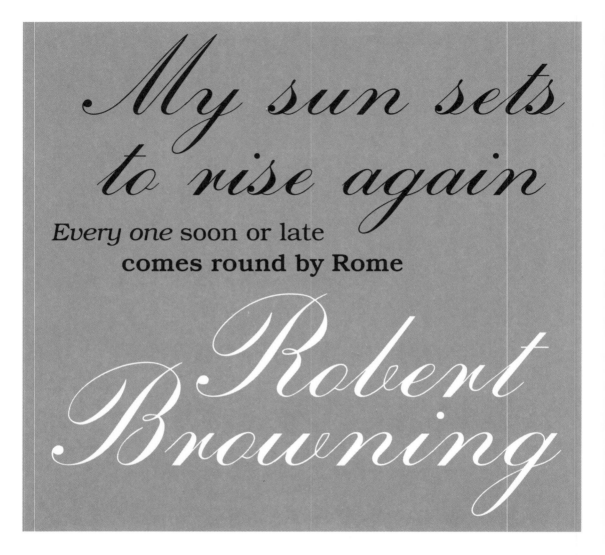

My sun sets to rise again

Every one soon or late comes round by Rome

Robert Browning

Monotype's Sackers English Script is a versatile Formal script face. It shouldn't be confused with Sackers Italian Script, which is slightly finer and somewhat more flamboyant, as you might expect from the naming choices, and is a better choice if the Victorian era is your visual goal. As an Old Style serif, ITC Bookman sits well with the traditional flavour of the script and adds to the historical pedigree despite both faces having relatively contemporary origins.

On this page

Sackers English Script

ITC Bookman

MESDAMES et MESSIEURS!

the Georgetown
FRENCH
MARKET

BOOK HILL'S SIGNATURE EUROPEAN OPEN AIR MARKET & SIDEWALK SALE

APRIL 19 & 20
10AM → 5PM
ALONG WISCONSIN AVENUE
FROM P STREET TO RESERVOIR ROAD

WWW.GEORGETOWNDC.COM

FASHION FINDS &
FRENCH FARE
QUAINT SHOPS, GALLERIES
AND LIVE MUSIC

UP TO 75% OFF
AT OVER 35 SHOPS
AND CAFÉS

PRESENTED BY THE GEORGETOWN BUSINESS IMPROVEMENT DISTRICT

GEORGETOWN
COME OUT AND PLAY
GEORGETOWNDC.COM
FACEBOOK | TWITTER | YOUTUBE

EVENT SPONSORS
Alliance Française
art Soirée
PASSPORT
TD Bank
The Georgetown Current

Client	The Georgetown Business Improvement District
Studio/ Designer	Fuszion/Rick Heffner
Web	fuszion.com
Principal typefaces	Knockout, Bodoni, Serifa Black

The spirit of the French Market, an annual spring event in Washington, D.C., is evoked through the use of faces which emulate the style of type popular during the Victorian era.

Principle #2 | Characters, glyphs and points

The size of a character can be expressed as either a body height or body width, although I tend to talk about body height and *glyph* width to help make a clearer distinction between the two values; in a proportional typeface the body height is constant but the glyph width varies constantly. Characters and glyphs are slightly different by the way; for example 'g' is a character but there may be more than one style of 'g' in a font, so each of those alternate characters is called a glyph.

Let's start with body height. When type was set in hot metal either by hand or by a device such as the Linotype line-casting machine, each glyph rested on a metal block – the body – consistently sized for each font. We talk about point size today as though it's the height of the glyphs but point size is actually an expression of the body height of a font, which is now a virtual area rather than a physical block of material. Understanding this contributes towards understanding why different typefaces set at the same point size don't always appear to be the same size.

The glyph width can be thought of as the width of the metal block that I mentioned earlier. Every separate glyph that appears as part of a font's character set will vary in width, and the *voice* of any one typeface is governed in part by how wide the glyphs are. For example, a significant difference in comparable glyph widths between differing typefaces will give greater emphasis to the wider typeface if both are similar in weight. There are practical considerations too of course; for example, if text must be set over a short measure a condensed weight or a font with narrow glyph widths would be an appropriate choice. Incidentally, avoid artificially condensing (or indeed expanding) a typeface because glyph shapes shouldn't be distorted; please use a proper condensed typeface.

Body height carries less importance when combining typefaces since line spacing (leading in traditional terminology or line feed as it is now called in our digital world) can be adjusted very easily and can be negative as well as positive. However, glyph width is an important visual cue for successful typeface pairing, especially if you are looking at two faces that are going to be used together at a similar x-height.

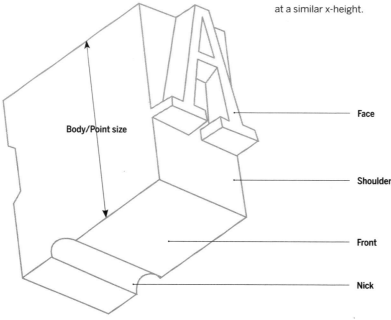

Body/Point size

Face

Shoulder

Front

Nick

Rag

Digital type still sits within a virtual body of space with the height corresponding to the point size. Glyph width varies constantly but the body height is constant for each font size.

gr gs g g g

Contemporary scripts are particularly well stocked with additional glyphs for each character to ensure links work convincingly. The example shown, The Carpenter, features several alternatives for 'g' as well as special ligatures for common linking pairs.

FESTE DES LEBENS UND DER KUNST

A significant TYPOGRAPHIC milestone

New meets *old*

Akzidenz Grotesk was one of the earliest Grotesque sans serif typefaces to be made available as a commercial release, emerging from the Berthold foundry in Berlin, Germany, in 1896. Its ubiquity at the time meant that it dominated the market for years and influenced many of the Neo-Grotesques that appeared during the 1950s. Eric Gill's Transitional serif Joanna appeared in 1930 and its simple lines pair well with Akzidenz, as does the contemporary face FF Scala.

On this page

Berthold Akzidenz Grotesk

Joanna MT

FF Scala

Mucha

Art Nouveau

A sans serif workhorse

Morris Fuller Benton

1904

The display face Arnold Boecklin, named after the Swiss painter Arnold Böcklin, is pretty much a one-hit wonder in that it's not much good for any uses outside the realms of its Art Nouveau roots. However, it does its intended job well and enjoyed a psychedelic revival during the 1960s. Its flamboyancy demands a very straightforward partner that won't vie for attention, so choose something like plain-talking News Gothic to maintain order.

On this page

Arnold Boecklin

News Gothic

DESTINY
what lies ahead
1927–1988
Arguably influenced by Futura's *geometry*

Futura, designed by Paul Renner in 1927, is the original and arguably most famous Geometric sans serif. It's certainly endured and is still popular after nearly ninety years of regular use, conjuring up the 1930s Bauhaus vibe perfectly, and Futura ND from Neufville is likely the most faithful interpretation of Renner's original design. Adrian Frutiger's Avenir addresses readability issues thrown up by Futura's strict geometry and works better at smaller sizes.

On this page

Futura ND
Avenir

DE STIJL
van Doesburg
Horizontal & vertical
Classic Eccentricity

Brown, designed by Aurèle Sack for Lineto and released between 2007 and 2011, is a Geometric sans serif with roots in the early twentieth century. Its single-storey 'a' and 'g' relate to Futura but it's not a revival; its proportions are less classical so character widths are more regular. To offset Brown's sterner qualities, try pairing it with Farnham, a 2004 Transitional serif from Christian Schwartz for Font Bureau inspired by eccentric eighteenth-century letterforms.

On this page

Brown
Farnham

Trick #3 | Hierarchy is important

It's rare for a layout to not require some degree of typographic hierarchy. Hierarchy introduces levels within the text; chapter headings, cross headings, captions and so on; and provides the reader with the signposts they need to successfully navigate their way through the layout. Point size and spacing are layout techniques that help to provide hierarchy, but there are a couple of equally important ways to achieve it that are linked to typeface choice – weight and form.

When you're selecting typefaces for a project, pay attention to the number of available weights in each typeface family. Contemporary typeface families regularly consist of multiple weights ranging from ultra thin to extra bold, while in the past a family would often contain just four weights: regular, regular italic, bold and bold italic. Often that's all you'll need but for more complex typographic layouts, such as directories or listings, a few extra weights will prove very useful. These can be weights within one family, or in combination from several different families.

Form refers to the glyph shapes of a typeface, particularly the lowercase glyphs, which display a greater level of variation than uppercase characters. By way of an example to illustrate the relevance of this, an expanded face, even when used at the same point size and visually similar weight to a face with a narrower glyph width, is likely to stand out and create hierarchy. Alternatively, a typeface that features open apertures and minimal contrast may not hold its own against another that features closed apertures and moderate contrast, since the latter may create more *colour* (see page 132).

Festival of the Arts
Music, Dance, Mime and Theatre
Tickets available from Uptown Bookshop or online

28 July to 3 August
11a.m. to 11p.m. • Midnight Friday and Saturday

Southdown Fields and Lakeside
www.musicdancemime.org

The text above displays several layers of hierarchy but all the fonts are from one family, Amplitude. The bold and extended weights draw the eye to the important information: what, when, where and website.

BAUHAUS
AUSSTELLUNG
August 15
Weimar

ITC Bauhaus interprets an early experimental alphabet, Universal, designed at the Bauhaus in 1925 by Herbert Bayer. ITC Bauhaus appeared in 1975 and proved popular at that time although, like many faces of their generation, its uses are now relatively limited and it's best used to evoke a contemporary 1970s–80s feel. Both FS Dillon and Colfax also reference the Rational letterforms of the 1920s and 1930s but add a twenty-first-century twist to the proceedings.

On this page
Bauhaus
FS Dillon
Colfax

BAYER

Russian Constructivism

BUNDESLAND

Saxony-Anhalt

Geometric sans serif FS Dillon from Fontsmith takes its inspiration from work created at the Bauhaus during the 1920s and 1930s. However, nuances such as the compact letterforms and larger x-height improve legibility and create opportunities for the face that older type can't successfully achieve – a general trait of twenty-first-century typeface designs. Pair it with Hoefler & Co.'s Idlewild or HVD Fonts Brandon Text to conjure up that distinctive 1930s feel.

On this page

FS Dillon

IDLEWILD

Brandon Text

Client	The German Printing Industry
Studio/Designer	Joost Schmidt
Principal typefaces	Akzidenz Grotesk, custom lettering

German journal Offset Buch und Werbekunst, *published in 1926, features a mixture of existing typefaces and hand-drawn custom lettering – a common practice at this time. Collection Merrill C. Berman*

Nord Express

Travel Glamour
Land, Sea & Air

The great commercial artist A. M. Cassandre designed Peignot for French foundry Deberny & Peignot in 1937. The letterforms are out-and-out Art Deco in style and there is no traditional lowercase; a mixture of lowercase and small caps are used instead, which restricts the face to display use. To continue the Art Deco theme try Neutraface 2 Condensed from House Industries, or use Avenir if a more straightforward text pairing is appropriate.

On this page

Peignot
Neutraface 2 Condensed
Avenir

Core Deco from S-Core belongs to the new generation of layered typefaces that can be combined to create multicolour glyphs, although separate fonts from the large family also work perfectly well in isolation. The face is clearly designed for display use and works well at larger sizes when built into composite headlines. Futura Condensed maintains the 1930s feel of this combination, with Idlewild from Hoefler & Co. adding a little timeless chic to the proceedings.

On this page

CORE DECO

Futura Condensed

IDLEWILD

Charles & Ray

Architectural
Universal

Eames Century Modern from House Industries takes the style of a Century Schoolbook and injects a lively dose of vivacity in tribute to the eponymous Charles and Ray, who contributed so much to the modern design aesthetic. It's both happy and functional with a flexible eighteen-weight family. To evoke the 1950s try pairing it with either Neue Helvetica or Univers, both famous Neo-Grotesque typefaces released to great acclaim in 1957.

On this page

Eames Century Modern
Neue Helvetica
Univers

Expatriate

PHARAOH

Contemporary classic

The latest news updated

Memphis predates mid-century Modern by about twenty years but it manages to give off a more Modernist aura than its close rival Rockwell; its stems and serifs are of equal weight and its letterforms feel slightly more polished than other Geometric slabs of the same period. The extensive Benton Sans family of regular, condensed and compressed styles revives News Gothic, bringing it into the present day without losing any of the classic feel of the original influence.

On this page

Memphis
Benton Sans
Benton Sans Extra Compressed

SWISS
Personified
Unrivalled
POPULARITY

There's little to be said about Helvetica that hasn't been said already and it's installed on everyone's PC. However, it can still look as stylish as ever (in the right hands) or as functional as necessary; it's good for logos, signage, packaging and on-screen graphics, in fact any type that requires a quiet consistency and an even colour. Ironically, it's weakest used in long passages of text due to its uniformity, but the huge range of styles offers a wealth of hierarchical possibilities.

On this page

Neue Helvetica
Neue Helvetica Condensed
Neue Helvetica Extended

Pragmatic
Rational
Functional
Beautiful

Akkurat, released in 2004 by Swiss foundry Lineto, is a kind of Helvetica on steroids. It successfully attempts to rationalise the letterforms of a Neo-Grotesque by reducing contrast and tightening up angles to the extent that it's practically a Geometric sans, but not quite. It's almost an affront to pair it with anything that might detract from its pure geometry but Transitional serif Arnhem's large x-height and clean functionality does work.

On this page

Akkurat
Arnhem

Trick #4 | How many fonts (or typefaces)?

The title of this trick forms a slightly loaded question as fonts and typefaces are different things although the terms are loosely interchangeable so it's worth reiterating their separate meanings by way of an example. Garamond Premier Regular is a typeface, but 12-point Garamond Premier Regular is a font; all the glyphs, including punctuation and symbols for a typeface at a specific point size and weight, make a single font.

Getting back to the question, the number of *fonts* you decide to use in a single layout depends on the complexity of the hierarchy required, and the number of *typefaces* you decide on for the same layout is governed by the amount of typographic personality you wish to input. I've provided one possible response to the question below – it demonstrates that the first typographic decision is often 'how many *typefaces* do I need', which in this case is two, a headline with attitude followed by a stylish sans serif with a sense of authority to offset the casual script. The decision about the fonts will form once you've read the text and ascertained the hierarchy, but you should always think about how many fonts you *might* need in terms of differing weights before you get too far into a layout, Some typeface families are larger than others, a fact that might influence your decisions.

Personality

HOW MANY TYPEFACES DO YOU REALLY NEED?

In most cases the answer is probably going to be no more than two or three at the most. One might be a typeface with a lot of character, like the casual script *The Carpenter*, which has been used for the headline above. Introducing several different faces to a layout can look messy and confusing, so pick a complementary face that has a good range of weights, like *FS Emeric* for example, with weights ranging from thin to **heavy**, making sure that there are corresponding *italic* weights – at least for the lighter weights that you might use for running text.

Bakelite

TRANSISTOR

Collectible

Valve Amp

The superellipse, a flat-sided oval, provides the basis for the round letterforms of Melior. Designed by Hermann Zapf in 1952, the face is a sound choice for setting text that references the 1950s–60s period, bringing to mind Ercol coffee tables and Eames wallpaper patterns. The form is more common to Grotesque and Neo-Grotesque sans serifs like Univers, making Melior a good pair for sans serifs of this style. Geometric sans like Forza also pair well with Melior.

On this page

Melior
Univers
Forza

If advertising art of the 1950s–60s is your thing, Ed Interlock should top your shopping list. Designed by Ed Benguiat and released by House Industries in 2004, the uppercase glyphs utilise over 1,400 ligatures to produce a vast range of interlocking character pairs. Neutraface Slab, another House Industries face, references modernist architectural lettering and provides a great foil for the animated Ed Interlock, as does the geometric precision of Eurostile.

On this page

Ed Interlock
Neutraface Slab
Eurostile
    Extended

Client	Billy Wilder, Allied Artists Picture Corporation
Studio/Designer	Saul Bass
Principal typefaces	Custom hand-drawn, Trade Gothic

Saul Bass's custom lettering indicates perfectly what Ed Benguiat aimed to achieve with his clever headline typeface Ed Interlock.

CALIFORNIA
Dreaming
HALLUCINOGENIC
Don't do drugs!

Mojo by Jim Parkinson takes its influence from the lettering style used by artists such as Wes Wilson and Victor Moscoso in the 1960s, and from early twentieth-century Viennese Secessionist artists like Alfred Roller. With legibility taking second place over style, a solid partner is needed for any accompanying text, and Akzidenz Grotesk fits the bill given its late nineteenth-century origins. Syntax's tactile Humanist sans qualities also offer a good fit.

On this page

MOJO

Syntax

Berthold Akzidenz Grotesk

EPHEMERA

Tambourine

SAN FRANCISCO

Turn On, Tune In, and Drop Out

Juniper has a distinct 1960s air about it but is in fact an Adobe Originals typeface designed by Joy Redick in 1990. As a revival of turn-of-the-century wood type it's in tune with Victorian styles which enjoyed a surge in popularity during the 1960s. Try pairing Juniper with a face like Neo-Humanist Sans FF Balance or the quirky Neo-Grotesque Antique Olive, which also feature the less common horizontal axis and reversed stress characteristics.

On this page

JUNIPER

FF Balance

Antique Olive

Principle #3 | Contrast

To talk of contrast in typographic terms can mean two things. First, it can reference the way that typefaces combined in a layout work together to create hierarchy. Second, it can describe the difference between the thickest and thinnest strokes of a glyph within a font's character set, or the difference in the stroke widths between all the glyphs of a given font. Ideally, one should consider both these points simultaneously when assembling typeface combinations.

The Canadian typographer Carl Dair (1912–1967) systematised a set of seven kinds of typographic contrast in his book *Design with Type*, first published in 1952: size, weight, structure, form, texture, colour and direction. These points address the way a chosen typeface can be treated as part of a layout; for example, a colour can be applied to any typeface of a suitable weight (very light typefaces being the possible exception) so is not necessarily an indicator of which typeface you might first choose. However, in the context of this book a few of these points are also key markers for successful typeface pairings.

Weight Using different weights as part of a typeface combination is one of the simplest ways to introduce contrast to a layout, be it for the needs of emphasis or purely for visual texture. Bear in mind that you don't have to use completely different typefaces for this since larger families will include a range of weights that may achieve the level of contrast you need. Try using weights that are at least two apart to achieve enough visible difference in the comparative stroke weights.

Form Look at the shapes of the uppercase and lowercase glyphs in a font – these define the contrast of form for a single typeface and will dictate the typographic 'colour' of a layout. In this context colour is defined as the tonal value of a block of text expressed as a grayscale.

Texture The above mentioned Form will help create the typographic texture in a layout alongside the way the type is arranged. For example, if you're looking for a tightly woven texture consider a condensed face (serif or sans serif) with a sturdily weighted stroke. Alternatively, if you'd prefer a lighter contrast look at serif faces that generate more white space between the characters when set as running text and are likely to have a degree of contrast in their strokes.

This last point leads us to contrast in individual glyphs of a font. If you take a look at an Old Style serif such as Bembo you'll notice that the difference in the thickest and thinnest parts of their strokes is moderate; in other words the typeface has moderate contrast. Compare this to a high-contrast Modern serif such as Bodoni. You'll see how combining either Bembo or Bodoni with a sans serif that has minimal or no contrast will produce very different results on the page or screen.

The large selection of weights provided in all of the Gotham typeface families will provide ample opportunity to create contrast in a layout. The sample above shows the heaviest and lightest, Gotham Black and Light.

Abc
Abc

The glyph shapes of Grotesque slabs Farao and Clarendon are very similar but the larger counters and apertures of Farao combined with a wider glyph width give it slightly lighter overall contrast.

Busdae non nis volorem. Perecti occaborro illoreseque est et dolut doluptio et omnimol lorrum inciendam ipic totat. Ant is re ea dolescipsa sedio ilignatque inia into del ium dollor apitas dere solorerum doluptatur, volo maiori quas ero minciature moditionse cus ipsam es aut quo el iundit, occabor re net reri bea sendignatio is aliquate sed quianditam ipsantiis essimol uptatium, quossinum quod quas mos illenihit veligent as int re dolupient. Consequae cus, ommodisini ut quo excereh endae.

Busdae non nis volorem. Perecti occaborro illoreseque est et dolut doluptio et omnimol lorrum inciendam ipic totat. Ant is re ea dolescipsa sedio ilignatque inia into del ium dollor apitas dere solorerum doluptatur, volo maiori quas ero minciature moditionse cus ipsam es aut quo el iundit, occabor re net reri bea sendignatio is aliquate sed quianditam ipsantiis essimol uptatium, quossinum quod quas mos illenihit veligent as int re dolupient. Consequae cus, ommodisini ut quo excereh endae.

The paragraph of dummy latin text above is set in Amplitude Condensed Regular, which produces a fairly dark colour on the page, whereas the more open glyphs of Neue Swift on the right feel more airy. Both samples are set at the same point size and leading.

Deconstruct

BASEL

Experimental

1970s DADA

The typefaces Base 9 and Base 12 were designed by Zuzana Licko of Emigre. They were first published in 1995 on the reverse of a poster promoting the faces and are highly representative of the experimental design approach that many type designers were taking at that time. Geometric sans serif faces (particularly those with narrow glyph widths) were much in favour during Postmodernism's heyday so try pairing with a face like FS Dillon from Fontsmith.

On this page

Base 9

Base 12

FS Dillon

Joshua Tree

Tehachapi

San Andreas Fault

Las Vegas Strip

Cholla, another Emigre face designed between 1998 and 1999 by Sibylle Hagmann takes its name from a species of cactus that grows in the Mojave Desert. The family was created for the Art Center College of Design in Pasadena and comprises a broad range of styles unified by the distinctive taper where bowls connect with stems. Look at pairing it with faces such as Eurostile Condensed or Forza, which features glyphs with similar shape characteristics.

On this page

Cholla Sans
Eurostile Condensed
Forza

Never Mind the Font

London

Calling

Blockhead

Typography dating from the late twentieth century often features widely spaced Geometric or Neo-Grotesque sans serif faces with an emphasis on condensed or expanded styles. The extensive range of choice within the Univers family provides an abundance of hierarchical options that will also inject plenty of colour into a layout. Try Memphis, a legible Geometric slab with Humanist inflections, for shout paragraphs or side notes.

On this page

Univers Ultra Condensed

Univers

Memphis

SANTA CRUZ

62,864

España

Hedonistic Tendency

Modern No. 216 is a 1982 Ed Benguiat typeface and combines the distinctive high contrast of a Didone-style face with sharp bracketed serifs reminiscent of a Glyphic serif. Recycling historical styles is a key trait of Postmodernism; Modern serifs fit with this visual ethos and so were used extensively during this period. Try pairing with architectural faces like Heron Sans Condensed or Neutraface Slab for a distinct contrast between fine and sturdy.

On this page

Modern No. 216
Heron Sans Condensed
Neutraface Slab Text

Trick #5 | Mixing serifs and sans serifs

Using a sans serif for headlines and a serif for running text is one of the oldest type tricks in the book, but there are a few other traits associated with serifs and sans serifs that might come in useful:

- Serif faces are able to convey a sense of history that extends back beyond the nineteenth century, so they potentially provide you with a greater range of contextual options.
- To the untrained eye, it can be easier to differentiate one serif typeface from another when used in combination than when presented with a group of sans serif faces.
- Sans serif faces can handle tighter inter-character spacing than serif faces, so are a good choice for space-saving and attention-grabbing headlines.
- If the required setting includes a lot of numbers, particularly set at a small point size, sans serif numerals are generally more legible.
- Sans serif typefaces are effective when used to provide emphasis because the characteristically minimal contrast of Gothic and Geometric sans serifs provides a darker typographic colour.

And of course there's the seemingly eternal argument about which is best for running text, a serif or a sans serif. For many years serifs were considered to be more legible because of the extra detail in the shapes of the glyphs; it was thought that serifs helped to guide one's eye along the line of text. This has now been disproven since we actually read using saccadic movements, meaning we tend to take in groups of words using rapid eye movements. It was also believed that sans-serif typefaces caused eye fatigue because of their monotone glyph shapes, but Grotesque and Humanist sans serif faces feature characteristics similar to those of Transitional serifs so this claim can't realistically be substantiated. In conclusion, it's really a case of choosing the typeface that suits the character of the project, basing your choices on your own visual assessment.

LISTEN UP
History is repeating itself

WEDGE
innovation
If it *feels* right, it *is* right!
The Dark Side

The appropriation of historical styles for use in a contemporary context is closely associated with the Postmodern movement and nineteenth-century Victorian revivals were popular with graphic designers throughout the 1980s and 1990s. Saracen is Hoefler & Co.'s wedge serif addition to *The Proteus Project* collection and its powerful presence works in accord with uncomplicated Frutiger or specialist narrow Geometric sans Heroic Condensed.

On this page

Saracen
Frutiger
Heroic Condensed

ImageWriter
Dots per Inch
Cleaner Act
PIXEL PERFECT

Emigre first designed the range of faces that included Emigre Fifteen as 72 dots per inch fonts for screen use and dot matrix printer output. However, using them at sizes far larger than their intended application on printed material is a visual hallmark of the Postmodern period. Adding the clean lines of Geometric sans like the display face MVB Solano Gothic or the elegant Colfax will offset any angular vulgarity by providing visual balance.

On this page

Emigre Fifteen
MVB Solano Gothic
Colfax

Client	Museum of Modern Art, New York
Studio/Designer	April Greiman
Web	aprilgreiman.com
Principal typefaces	Modula, Emperor

April Greiman is a pioneer of digital graphic design – one of the great innovators. The Modern Poster, *designed in 1988, features coarse-resolution fonts with visible pixellation which were typical of the period.*

ARTIFACT

THE CULTURAL HERITAGE OF A NATION

American Signwriter

The Declaration of Independence

The term Americana carries with it a sense of vintage culture and Jim Parkinson's Modesto, first released in 2000 and subsequently expanded into a larger family of styles, references the handmade feel of vernacular American sign writing brilliantly well. It looks like a display face but works well as a text face too. Adobe Caslon, with its close ties to nineteenth-century American colonisation, also provides a sound visual pairing for this characterful Glyphic serif.

On this page

Modesto
Adobe Caslon

Republican

Abraham Lincoln

The 16th President

Ford's Theatre

For many years a significant problem has plagued designers who like to use Clarendon-style Slab serifs in their work – no italic weights! In fact a general limitation of weight options can severely hamper a Slab serif's versatility, so Hoefler & Co. designed the twelve-style Sentinel family. It feels both fresh and traditional and will pair well with some Transitional serifs as well as Geometric sans serifs such as Gotham or Gotham Narrow.

On this page

Sentinel
Gotham Narrow

Empire State

Steel girders

An American Cultural Icon

One hundred and three storeys

Heron Serif, designed by Cyrus Highsmith for Font Bureau in 2012, instantly conjures up a sense of hard work and even tougher workers with its very low contrast and tight glyph widths. It feels almost architectural and its moderate x-height feels taller than it actually is. Try it with the unusual Freight Micro family from GarageFonts, and be sure to select the correct optical sizes (Big, Micro or Text) for smaller text setting or larger headlines.

On this page

Heron Serif

Heron Serif Condensed

Freight Micro

Freight Text

If you want to create realistic-looking woodblock settings there are several good options now available, one of them being Eveleth, released by Yellow Design Studio in 2014. There are three styles to choose from; clean, dot and slant successfully replicate inked texture, and a shadow layer can also be added beneath as separate text. Older faces such as 1906's Century Old Style or the more contemporary but retro-styled Bureau Grot will pair nicely.

On this page

EVELETH
Century Old Style
Bureau Grot

This town ain't big enough for the both of us

Thankfully, these days a positive approach to diversity among social classes is high on the agenda for many people and it's a good idea to follow a similar avenue when it comes to typeface combinations. Relatives like to stick together, of course, so there's no issue combining fonts from the same typeface family, but pairing faces from different families of the same classification, particularly if the typefaces are of the seriffed variety, may not work out too well. This is particularly pertinent for typefaces with a heap of personality because they'll evidently clash; for example, try putting Grotesque slabs **Clarendon** and **Farao** together and you'll see what I mean. They're both great typefaces that were designed one hundred and fifty years apart but they need to be left to their own devices or they'll come to blows.

Bringing together similarly classed sans serif faces is arguably a little less contentious but, if you choose to try this, it's still wise to ensure that they're different enough to make the combination worthwhile. For example, Geometric sans **Futura** and **Brown** (which is influenced by Futura) are very similar so there's no point in using them together but **Brown** paired with **Heroic Condensed** used for the headline might work for the right kind of project. Either way, a generous mixture of class and culture makes for an interesting gathering, be it between people or typefaces.

A HEROIC HEADLINER with a great support act

Metroscript, designed by Michael Doret of Alphabet Soup in 2006, is an out-and-out celebration of the hand-lettering styles of the early twentieth century, with its contextual alternative glyphs and a selection of swashes and tails. Vitesse from Hoefler & Co. feels very twenty-first century but somehow maintains a retro aesthetic simultaneously, while Font Bureau's Amplitude with its huge x-height will also pair successfully with the flamboyant script.

On this page

Metroscript

Vitesse

Amplitude

New York

Manhattan

Wall Street

Elegant Brownstone Townhouse

Since its 2000 release, Hoefler & Co.'s Gotham, designed by Tobias Frere-Jones, has become *the* American sans serif. Inspired by the lettering on Manhattan's Port Authority Bus Terminal, it famously appeared on Barack Obama campaign posters and the inscription on the cornerstone of One World Trade Center. Its commanding presence demands a hard working partner, so try Mercury Text, a high-performance Old Style serif also from Hoefler & Co.

On this page

Gotham

Mercury

Client	Old 97's
Studio	Lure Design/ Paul Mastriani, Jeff Matz
Web	www.luredesigninc.com
Principal typefaces	Headlined, Belizio Bold

Old 97's are an alternative country band from Dallas, Texas, recognised as pioneers of the alt-country movement. The retro styling of their tour poster echoes the ethos of their musical style.

The sensual meandering of Font Bureau's Tangier, designed by Richard Lipton on 2010, will certainly help to conjure a steamy tropical flavour. This is despite the fact that it's actually a Formal calligraphic script, designed in part for elegant space-saving titling applications. When text setting is required, the calligraphic roots of TypeTogether's Pollen or Adobe's Cronos will blend perfectly with Tangier's curves, adding personality and charm to the mix.

On this page

Tangier
Pollen
Cronos

Rumba

Afro-Cuban

Guaguancó

Before Castro

Laura Meseguer's Rumba, released in 2005, comes in three varieties – Rumba Small for text, Rumba Large for headlines and the highly expressive Rumba Extra, which fairly dances across the page in an imitation of its namesake. When set with cheery calligraphic faces such as the Contemporary serif FS Olivia from Fontsmith, or Doko from Urdt, the party is guaranteed to continue late into the night.

On this page

Rumba
FS Olivia
Doko

ARCTIC
North Pole
Rockhopper
Antarctic

Humanist sans Inagur from Linotype features outwardly curving stems that somehow make the glyphs feel as if they're puffing themselves up like small birds trying to keep warm on a cold winter's morning. An unusual face like this requires a sensible partner and FF Dax fits the bill, as does TheMix. Both of these faces have character shapes that harmonise well with those of Inagur, but lack the inflated strokes, making them a better choice for smaller text.

On this page
Inagur
FF Dax
TheMix

FROZEN
to the bone
Progressive Glaciation
Hypothermic Reaction

Display face Aniuk, released in 2010 by Austrian foundry Typejockeys, is very much a face designed to go large. All five available weights are fairly full-bodied and the gently curving strokes are somehow reminiscent of snowdrifts and ski jumps – at least they look that way to me! To offset the undulating slopes of Aniuk, try it alongside a spiky Contemporary face like Neue Swift with its icicle-like wedge serifs and crisp character shapes.

On this page

Aniuk
Neue Swift

Principle #4 | Apertures and counters

Anatomically, apertures and counters occupy similar ground; in fact, some would say they are interchangeable and mean pretty much the same thing. However, a distinction between the two can and should be made because it helps to describe specific glyph features more precisely.

An aperture is the opening between the interior white space and the exterior of a glyph. The clearest examples are the partially closed negative space in the upper portion of a double-storey lowercase 'a', and the similar space in the lower portion of a lower-case 'e'. The term can also be applied to the space formed inside a lowercase 'n', both the upper- and lower-case 'c', the negative areas in the upper and lower portions of an 's' and so on. As I mentioned above, these can also legitimately be called counters, as any reference work will show, but I prefer to think of these partially closed areas as apertures.

The distinction between an aperture and a counter can be seen as how *closed* the space is and what shape it is, so a counter is the enclosed circular or curved space within an 'o', the upper portion of a 'p' or 'g', the lower portion of a 'b' or 'd' and so on. Counters don't have to be closed; **Fedra Serif** is an example of a typeface that bucks the trend as it features open bowls on the lower-case roman (but not italic) 'b' and the 'p', and on the '6' and '9', but this kind of feature isn't terribly common. This lends support to the practice of using duel sub-categories of counter, closed-counters and open-counters, with closed-counters being the most prevalent.

It's helpful to look at the shapes of both apertures and counters when combining typefaces because the relative size and shape of these anatomical features will have a bearing on visual compatibility. For example, contemporary serifs often feature a large x-height and

Aperture

Counter

apertures that are more open. Trying to visually balance a typeface with large counters to one with smaller counters could mean that the former ends up looking too small in a layout while the latter looks too large.

Finally, don't confuse apertures and counters with loops and bowls because these are strokes, and remember that the small negative area that appears in the upper portion of a lowercase 'e' is sometimes referred to as the *eye* but is basically a counter.

Bowl

Loop

Yoga Sans (on the left) has a moderate x-height that is still considerably larger than the very small x-height of Mrs Eaves on the right. Any attempt to match their x-heights in a layout will result in the latter looking far too large in comparison to the former.

Above these examples, FS Olivia Pro has been used to provide a visual example of both a bowl and a loop. Take care not to confuse these anatomical features with apertures and counters.

It's all too easy to simply choose big powerful typefaces to achieve a masculine quality with type, but that's not the full story. However, in the above example the choices couldn't be any more punchy. Both are Hoefler & Co. typefaces; Leviathan is a Gothic sans serif and part of *The Proteus Project* collection of nineteenth-century style faces, while the hugely successful Gotham has more than enough power to stand up to Leviathan's mighty presence.

On this page

Leviathan

Gotham Condensed

Gotham

Ringside
Second's Out
Sugar Ray
Pound-for-Pound

The idea of a large typeface *family* is a relatively new concept. Traditionally, typefaces evolved organically in relation to whatever use was required of them, but now the realisation that a fully formed family of styles will provide a multitude of hierarchical possibilities is widespread. Hoefler & Co.'s Knockout is a thirty-two-style family that covers all the bases, and pairing it with a sturdy Slab serif such as Sentinel means this combination will never punch below its weight.

On this page

Knockout
Sentinel

Colfax, an oval Geometric sans serif released by the Process Type Foundry in 2012, mixes contemporary looks with traditional influence to produce a face full of quiet strength and subtle poise. This twelve-font family, comprising six weights of roman and italic from thin to black, is designed to achieve perfect overall contrast by combining weights that are two apart, for example medium plus black. This 'rule' is a useful principle to bear in mind generally.

On this page

Colfax

EDIFICE

You can't miss me!

Capable and kind

Handy around the house

Acropolis, another of the four components of Hoefler & Co.'s *The Proteus Project*, creates a massive presence on the page with its bevel-edged letterforms. This typeface style is known as Grecian, hence the naming choice for the face, and once again there is a very useful and attractive italic, which is often missing from other big display faces of this kind. Try pairing it with Fedra Sans, which has diamond-shaped tittles to match with Acropolis Italic.

On this page

Acropolis
Fedra Sans

FS Emeric, designed by Phil Garnham at Fontsmith, is a Humanist sans serif that feels full of life. It makes a very bold statement regardless of the choice of weight and is both steadfastly solid and light on its feet at the same time, opening up a very wide range of possibilities for the twenty-two styles included in the family. Try pairing it with Humanist serif Cala to maintain a feeling that combines modernity with dependability.

On this page

FS Emeric
Cala

VROOM!

It's a Mustang

Mine's an Aston Martin

V8 Supercharger

Speed Trap

Freight Micro, released by GarageFonts in 2004, is comprised of specific optical sizes or styles for particular uses, in this case Freight Text, Display and Big as well as Micro, which sits at the core of the family. It's an extremely legible and stylishly punchy face, which is unusual enough to pair with lots of different styles. Stylish Transitional serif Le Monde Livre adds some extra gravitas while innovative Humanist sans Auto maintains the energetic atmosphere.

On this page

Freight Micro
Le Monde Livre
Auto

Trick #7 | Weight problems?

Some projects are clear right from the off; you'll be given the content in its complete form at the start of the schedule and the author of the text is absolutely certain that they'll not want to introduce any subcategories further down the line. But how often does that happen? Not often enough is probably the closest generic answer to that question but it's something that goes with the territory. So, what's a good strategy for typeface choices if you think there's a likelihood that a project's typographic requirements are likely to increase during the design and layout process?

There are a lot of type families out there with weight ranges limited to just four: regular, italic, bold and bold italic (see also hierarchy on page 46). That's fine if you only need one level of heading but what if you discover you need three or four halfway through the project? This is particularly pertinent to the choice of typeface for the running text because adding different faces into the mix to deal with cross headings or call-out paragraphs can begin to look messy. Contemporary releases of new typefaces (and revivals of older styles) tend to feature a broader range of available weights so always consider your options in this area before cementing your final choices.

FS Emeric from Fontsmith is a superfamily with eleven weights, all with a corresponding italic. If you think you'll need several contrasting weights for a project, a large typeface family will ensure that you'll not run out of options.

Thin
Extra light
Light
Book
Regular
Core
Medium
Semi Bold
Bold
Extra Bold
Heavy

Kinsfolk

Loving partner

Teenage Kids

A happy tribe

Auto is an unusual and innovative family of typefaces, released in 2005 by collaborative foundry Underware. It's a Humanist sans with obvious calligraphic qualities pared down to create the roman weights, but the real innovation comes in the shape of three different italic styles: Auto 1, 2 and 3. The expressive qualities of the italic increases with the number – Auto 1 takes a relatively standard form, while Auto 3 features extravagant swashes and tails.

On this page

Auto Regular

Auto 1 Italic

Auto 2 Italic

Auto 3 Italic

Geezer

Big Guy

Salt of the Earth

Chip off the Old Block

If there's one Grotesque slab that always makes itself heard, it's Giza. Emulating the Slab serif faces popular in nineteenth-century England, Font Bureau's 1994 release comprises a range of weights running from relatively subtle to monumentally enormous. This typeface makes powerful headlines but can never work as text so try pairing it with a legible Slab that works at smaller sizes, perhaps Sentinel or TheSerif.

On this page

Giza

Sentinel

TheSerif

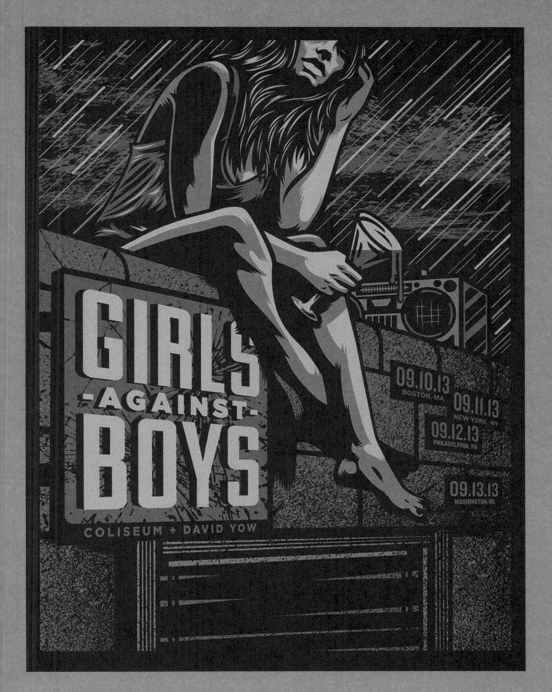

Client	Girls Against Boys
Studio/Designer	Rockets are Red
Web	rockets-are-red.com
Principal typefaces	Duke, Gotham, Knockout

This three-colour screen-printed poster for the reunion tour of indie band Girls Against Boys employs tough sans serif headline faces that fall in line with the tough but poignant urban setting.

Fontsmith has a penchant for delivering typefaces that are cheery, poetic and personable, and Eleni Beveratou's FS Olivia is no exception. The unusually curved legs, tails and diagonal strokes are very sensual yet the Glyphic-style counters rub up against the curves like an eager suitor. The finely drawn curves of Flirt Script pile on the femininity of this combination, and for a functional Geometric sans Brandon Text feels surprisingly at home.

On this page

FS Olivia

Flirt Script

Brandon Text

Well hello!

Care for a coffee

or

cocktails?

I'm having a Mai Tai

Archer, released by Hoefler & Co. in 2008 after developing it for *Martha Stewart Living* magazine, takes a Geometric slab and injects a healthy dose of friendly charm. The ball terminals that appear mainly on the lowercase characters are key to this effect. The extremely beautiful SangBleu might fight for headline space but could work in a layout with extra call-out elements, and the functional but graceful Verlag makes a good partner for text setting.

On this page

Archer
Sang Bleu
Verlag

Strawberry preserve

Barbecue

Your dinner's in the dog

Zuzana Licko's Filosofia, released by Emigre in 1996, is a Bodoni-inspired Didone with contemporary twists thrown in to render a friendly and informal face that drops sharp serifs in favour of rounder ends and a few cheeky ball terminals. Its fairly limited range of weights might encourage the addition of a comparable face like Abril Text, which offers greater choice for running text, and Archer may prove useful for other miscellaneous text that has to work at small sizes.

On this page

Filosofia
Abril Text
Archer

Ciao!

So good of you to drop by

I wasn't expecting you

Love the shirt...

Lust Display from Positype is a sexy no-holds-barred display face that demands to be used at very large point sizes. In fact the designer, Neil Summerour, provides a humorously worded warning in his online description about the supermodel propensities of this sensuous typeface. The gentler form of Monotype's cut of Walbaum provides a calming foil for approachable running text, or try FS Lola if a cleaner modern look is required.

On this page

Lust Display
Walbaum MT
FS Lola

C.E.O.

Power dress

The Boss

Member of the Board

Hoefler and Co.'s Chronicle, available in both display and text style, was begun in 2002 as a project to create a Transitional serif in the Scotch style that would perform well under punishing print conditions, retaining the delicate details found in the serifs and tails. The result incorporates four different grades of text weights for use with different print environments. A Geometric sans such as Gotham pairs extremely well with Chronicle.

On this page

Chronicle Display
Chronicle Text
Gotham

STYLE
Art Director
New York
Fashion Week
Catwalk sensation

HTF Didot from Hoefler & Co. is unquestionably one of the most delicately nuanced Modern serifs available today. This is due to the availability of seven optical sizes for each style that thin down strokes and serifs incrementally as the assigned optical size increases. This way, details remain fine at larger printed sizes. An elegant Didone requires an elegant partner and Sentinel manages this despite its Slab serif classification.

On this page
HTF Didot
Sentinel

All of **these fonts** are set **at the** same point size to demonstrate **how** x-height varies between different TYPEFACES.

Body height is discussed on pages 36–37 including the relationship between body height and point size. Point size is an expression of the body height of a font rather than the size of the glyphs; in the days of metal type the body was the physical block that held each glyph, and this has been carried over to digital fonts in the form of a defined area. The body height of this virtual area is constant at every given point size, while the width varies with the width of the font's glyphs. On the other hand, glyph heights are consistent between fonts within a typeface family (i.e. 10pt Garamond Regular and 10pt **Garamond Bold** share the same glyph height) but vary between fonts of the same point size from *different* families.

So what are the implications of this in practice? Basically, if you set two typefaces together that are the same point size they will appear to be different sizes. Let's use Mrs Eaves and **Frutiger** as an example to demonstrate this principle. **Frutiger** will look larger when set at the same point size as Mrs Eaves because it was designed with a large x-height compared to Mrs Eaves' particularly small x-height. To pair two or more typefaces in a layout where they need to appear similarly sized, you must visually match the x-heights rather than simply set them at the same point size. Therefore, it makes sense to look at fonts that already display similar x-height characteristics as part of your initial trawl for choices.

SPEND
Boutique
Store
Emporium
All a girl could want!

Luxury Platinum from House Industries is one-third of a display face family (the others are Luxury Gold and Luxury Diamond) that set out to celebrate the lettering style so often found on luxury goods packaging such as perfume or fashion accessories. The Humanist leanings of Syntax, with its angled terminals, makes a good partner for accompanying text, and some vintage fun can be had by adding a Casual script like Sign Painter House Casual to the set.

On this page

LUXURY
PLATINUM
Syntax
Sign Painter House Casual

FREE
to do what you want!
Live your life
Make your own rules

The overtly feminine and very beautiful Liza family from Underware takes full advantage of OpenType architecture, producing convincing 'hand lettered' script through the use of over 4,000 glyphs that combine for optimal effect. Contemporary serif Eureka, with its humanistic leanings and long extenders, sits comfortably alongside Causal script faces, and Whitney's open apertures and angled terminals bring just enough personality to the table.

On this page

LIZA CAPS PRO
Liza Text Pro
Eureka
Whitney

Client	786 The Fragrance
Studio/Designer	Hype Type Studio/Paul Hutchinson
Web	hypetype.co.uk
Principal typefaces	Luxury Gold, Helvetica

Paul Hutchinson's choice of Luxury Gold as the principal typeface for 786 The Fragrance's packaging is perfect – a fine example of a face used exactly as its designer intended.

Farao

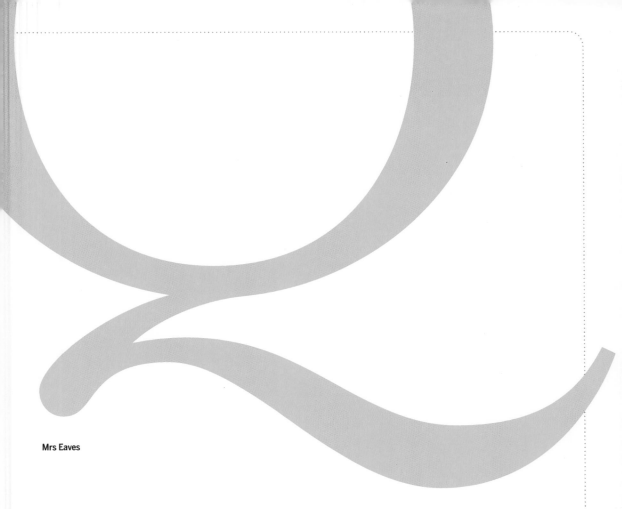

Mrs Eaves

The typographic terms 'leg' and 'tail' can be confusing because there's a degree of overlap, so here's a little more detail about the separate meanings. The lower downwards sloping stroke of both the uppercase and lowercase 'K' and the corresponding lower stroke on the upper-case 'R' (excluding any serif that may appear at the terminal) is the leg. The curved stroke that either sits on or extends below the baseline of the uppercase 'Q' is known as the tail, but it's also correct to refer to a tapered stroke at the end of a leg as a tail, and it's worth mentioning that the descenders of the lowercase 'j' and 'y' can be referred to as tails, particularly if they're prominently curved.

When identifying typefaces that you've seen in use and would like to combine with other faces in your existing collection, leg and tail shapes are two of the most useful features to examine, particularly if you've narrowed your decision down to several faces that look similar. The elegance and flair of a luxuriously extended tail on the upper-case 'Q' of a typeface such as Adobe Caslon, or a richly decorative tail of the kind that appears on the corresponding glyph of Mrs Eaves can really set a design apart. An upturned tail completing the leg of a Grotesque slab-serif's uppercase 'R' is the equivalent of a typographic smile, and the choice of either a curved or straight leg can radically alter the tone of your text. Bear in mind that, if you've already chosen a text face with tall ascenders, you should look carefully at how far tails extend below the baseline of your headline typeface in order to avoid awkward clashes.

Mean Streets

Dark Entries

Inner-City

Ladies of the Night

Quadon, designed by Rene Bieder, is a contemporary take on the Slab serif style that's tough enough to walk the streets with impunity but still look cool at the club. An extensive family of nine weights combines with a decent collection of alternative glyphs, making this a very versatile face. The superellipse letterforms pair up well with the similar shapes found in Forza, or you could try Meta Serif if your subject matter is of a slightly more serious tone.

On this page

Vitesse
Forza
Meta Serif

LONDON

The Square Mile

32 Boroughs

Inner Temple

This combination of fairly elderly typefaces is definitely historical, traditional urban as opposed to urban cool. Glyphic serif Albertus is used on all street signage throughout the City of London, the area within Greater London known as the Square Mile. Gill Sans is a Humanist sans serif and Joanna a Transitional serif, but both were designed by Eric Gill whose background as an inscriptional lettering artist brought a degree of Glyphic quality to his faces.

On this page

Albertus

Gill Sans

Joanna MT

TENEMENT
Land & Rent
Graffiti
Seedy sidestreets

You may accuse me of choosing Urban Grotesk here because it's got the word 'urban' in its name, but for once the name fits the face. Suitcase Type Foundry's Grotesque sans achieves an architectural feel not dissimilar to Gotham's, and partners well with the Contemporary Humanist Slab serif Soho, which injects a bit of texture into the mix. To really liven things up, add Process Type Foundry's Casual script Pique with its overtones of the graffiti artist's marker-pen 'tag'.

On this page
Urban Grotesk
Pique
Soho

If your current project needs to portray a specific feeling, take care not to confuse the reader by introducing any typographic mood swings. Type, along with colour, is one of the best tools in the box for mood creation but the technique really only works if the mood is focused; putting a typeface with a bold temper in the same layout as one inclined to light good humour is probably going to create a bit of a scene.

Happy!

if not exuberant...

So, when mood is your top priority think about one stand-out typeface that will get the idea across. This might be the headline font on a magazine page or a main title as part of a poster layout, but it could equally be the typeface you choose for the running text if that's the principal content of your layout. Whatever the case, find the typeface that really summons up the mood you want to portray, then combine it with other faces that either support the mood or are neutrals that won't dilute the impact of your signature typeface. And remember, if the typeface is too moody and draws more attention to itself than it should, your readers might get irritated and leave the room.

Studio Space

Atelier workshops

BESPOKE

BOUTIQUE

Downtown

We're heading back to the printers' district with this combination that mixes tradition with modernity. Amasis is a fresh Humanist slab, designed by Ron Carpenter for Monotype in 1990, that eschews the stricter geometry of many other slab serif faces. Its moderately tall x-height pairs well with Geometric sans Colfax, and for a little Victorian retro fun you could look at a face like Brandon Printed, an eroded letterpress-style face with four variations for each glyph.

On this page

Amasis

BRANDON PRINTED

Colfax

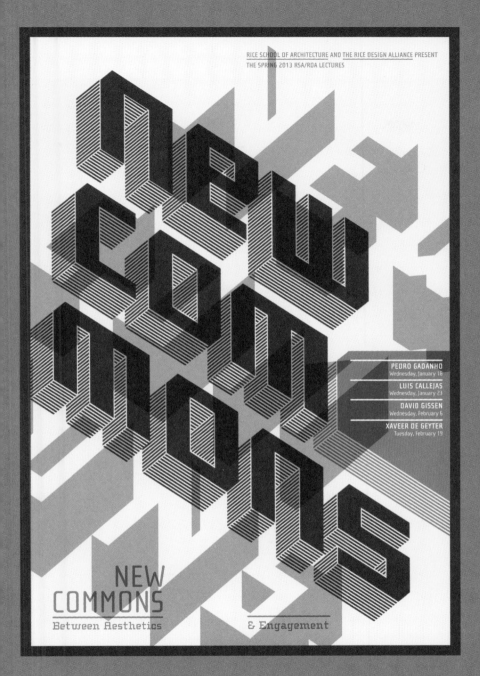

Client	Rice School of Architecture
Studio/Designer	CORE Design Studio
Web	coredesignstudio.com
Principal typefaces	Cholla Sans, SlabStruct Too, Rhohan Regular, xtrude Regular.

This poster by Houston's Core Design Studio is one element of the material created to promote a lecture series by Rice Design Alliance and Rice School of Architecture. Geometric Cholla Sans provides a slightly softer partner to the strongly architectural feel of the other faces used.

Regional

Outlying district

Coffee morning

Rustic pursuits
at the Village Hall

The provinces of a town, or even a country, are occasionally seen as less sophisticated than the city but this is usually an unjustified view. Provincial towns are just as likely to mix sophistication with tradition, as does the combination of Lineto's Geometric sans Brown with Adobe's charming Humanist serif Brioso, which brings a calligraphic flavour to a contemporary face featuring four optical variations for captions, text, subheads and display.

On this page

Brown

Brioso Display

Brioso

The Times

Broadsheet or Red Top

LATE NIGHT AT THE OFFICE?

The 7.53

At a certain time the world over, people crowd onto trains and head from the suburbs into the city for the daily commute. Until recently, a sea of newsprint would be a common sight but these days smartphones and tablets seem omnipresent. However, the combination of the highly recognisable Transitional serif Times New Roman with a workhorse sans serif like Franklin Gothic will for me always bring forth memories of a grey Monday morning on the underground.

On this page

Times New Roman
Franklin Gothic

Arts & Crafts

Charming Muse

Afternoon Squire

Stylish oldie

Eric Gill spent many years living a provincial (and indeed unconventional) life in Ditchling, East Sussex and Speen in Buckinghamshire. Gill Sans carries with it much of the British charm and quirkiness found in these locations but it also feels very sure and stable, as does Mercury with its moderately Glyphic serifs, which are quite sharp for an Old Style face. With similar x-heights the two make an unlikely but harmonious pair.

On this page

Gill Sans
Mercury Display
Mercury Text

Colourless SAFEHOUSE Weekender *Spring in your step*

Since its original appearance in the late 1940s, Trade Gothic has always been regarded as a down-to-earth typeface with a broad range of uses. This is all very well but hardworking can sometimes translate as boring and it will always benefit from a visit by a livelier face. Archer's origins lie in the world of lifestyle magazine publishing but it manages to avoid following the homeware-obsessed flock by being pretty but not empty-headed.

On this page

Trade Gothic
Trade Gothic
Bold Condensed No. 20
Archer

US-50

The Loneliest Road

Coast to Coast

Get Your Kicks!

Backbone of America

Interstate was developed during the 1990s by Tobias Frere-Jones and is closely related to Highway Gothic, the informal name for the fonts used on road signage throughout the US and in many other parts of the world. Its optimal use for signage is offset by a number of refinements that also make it suitable for text setting, but you may want to try it as a headline face with Whitney, also by Frere-Jones, used for text since the letterforms of the two are very similar.

On this page

Interstate
Whitney

Optimist Mustard On the up! A face full of hope

Fontsmith's Humanist sans serif FS Emeric is full of energy and drive, like an enthusiastic young job seeker striving to become the next chief executive. On first meeting it comes across as a classic hardworking sans but there are beautifully subtle touches within the individual letterforms that raise its game and invite us to make the most of the possibilities offered by the twenty-two weights within the FS Emeric family.

On this page
FS Emeric

PROSPER
personnel
HARD WORK
Wolf from Your Door

Clear Sans, created by Positype's Neil Summerour, was designed to fill a gap. Summerour felt that too many Geometric sans faces drawn for display use lacked personality and wanted to introduce some of the warmth back into a face that reflected hand-drawn qualities alongside the precision of a modern digital font. It still manages to feel hardworking however, and sits nicely against a Contemporary Slab serif such as Soho.

On this page
Clear Sans
Soho

Newsworthy
Correspondent
DIPLOMATIQUE
SMALL CHANGE
Ragged Footnote

Originally commissioned for French newspaper *Le Monde*, Porchez Typofonderie's Le Monde offers four different styles: Journal, Livre, Sans and Courrier. The thinking behind the styles Journal and Livre is smart; optical sizing means Journal is best for text set at or below 10 points, while Livre, with its slightly smaller x-height, is better for larger setting. A narrow sans serif like Benton Sans Condensed will complement the narrow width of all Le Monde's styles.

On this page

Le Monde Livre
Le Monde Journal
Benton Sans Condensed

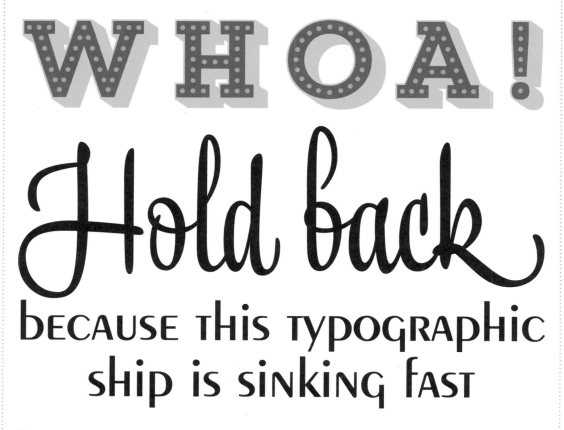

WHOA! *Hold back* BECAUSE THIS TYPOGRAPHIC ship is sinking fast

The most successful typeface pairings rely on a combination of acquired knowledge and a savvy approach to graphic design; it's simple enough to put typefaces together until you feel something looks right (and if this works for you, that's fine) but it's better to have some idea of where you're heading before you set out.

With that thought in mind, try to hold back on your combination choices a little and resist the temptation to simply pick faces that are obviously different, or just ones that you especially like. Think things through first by taking a look at individual faces in isolation in order to appreciate their distinct qualities before you introduce them to their new friends, bearing in mind that complete opposites don't always attract. One thing is certain – wildly contrasting combinations thrown together without reason are worse than those that don't contrast enough.

Having said that, and risking accusations of being contradictory, there may of course be times when wildly contrasting typefaces are just the ticket. Typography is by nature an unpredictable venture (despite what some traditionalists might try to tell you) and sometimes odd bedfellows work surprisingly well. But generally speaking, the best typeface combinations are built around harmony rather than discord.

We're at the market with this combination – think fruit and vegetables laid out with their handwritten price labels on metal spikes. Studio Slant from House Industries is unusual for a Casual script because it slants backwards; most are forwards leaning or occasionally upright, and it's a great celebration of a classic handwritten sign style. The calligraphic qualities of Humanist sans Cronos or the quirkiness of Freight Micro pair well with this unusual script.

On this page

Studio Slant

Cronos

Freight Micro

STYLE
Art Direct
Bombshell
Pretty in Pink

Print magazines remain hugely popular despite the surge in tablet use, and their design relies heavily on intelligent typeface choices. HTF Didot was created by Hoefler and Co. for *Harper's Bazaar* and its six styles with seven optical sizes per style mean that those delicate serifs will always look just right. Try pairing it with OurType's Transitional serif Arnhem, an attractive newspaper face that's also perfect for setting running text in magazines of all types.

On this page
HTF Didot
Arnhem

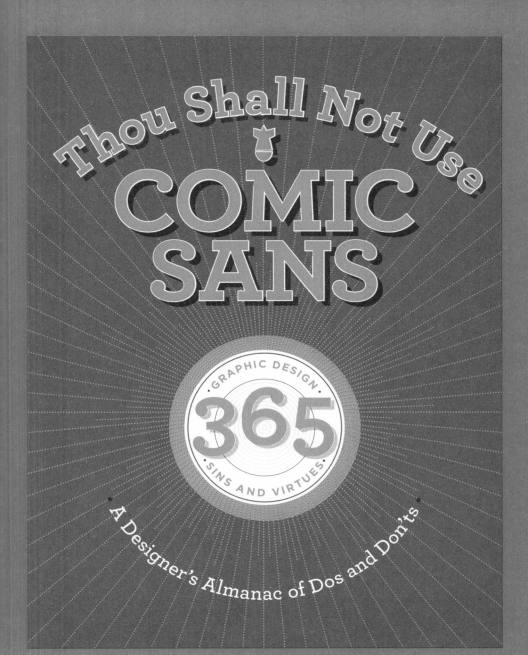

Thou Shall Not Use COMIC SANS

GRAPHIC DESIGN · 365 · SINS AND VIRTUES

A Designer's Almanac of Dos and Don'ts

Client	Quid Publishing
Studio/Designer	Tony Seddon
Web	www.tonyseddon.com
Principal typefaces	Archer, Gotham, Rians Dingbats

Commercial publishing project Thou Shall Not Use Comic Sans *approaches the subject of 'graphic design sins and virtues' with a mixture of fact-based advice and conversational humour. The cheerful yet disciplined letterforms of Geometric slab Archer help to echo the tone of the content, ably backed by Geometric sans Gotham.*

Principle #6 | Ascenders and descenders

Ascenders and descenders are the parts of lowercase glyphs that extend either above the x-height or below the baseline of a font. There are no hard and fast rules about how long an ascender or descender should be in comparison to the x-height or cap-height; this is a decision taken by the designer based on a combination of the visual and practical requirements intended for the typeface.

Let's take a look at ascenders first. The upper portion of certain glyphs – 'b', 'd', 'h' and so on – rises to an invisible line known as the ascender line. This line shouldn't be confused with the cap-height, which may or may not correspond; ascender lines sometimes sit ever so slightly higher to create the optical illusion that the tops of the glyphs visually align with the cap-height. In some cases the ascender line is noticeably higher, a feature that can aspire to create an elegant aesthetic for the typeface.

Pollen

Descender lengths are not tied proportionately to ascender heights. Contemporary typeface designs tend towards a larger x-height and more modest extenders (the collective term for ascenders and descenders). However, take a look at typefaces based on the earliest roman forms, such as **Adobe Jenson** or Centaur, and you'll see that the relative proportions of the extenders and the x-height are closer, with the body height split roughly into thirds: one-third ascender, one third x-height and one-third descender. This tends to make typefaces designed with these proportions look relatively small in the body, an important consideration in terms of how a face of this kind will combine with a more contemporary type family.

On a closing note, perhaps the most practical point to consider for typefaces with long ascenders and descenders is that lines of text often look better if they are spaced quite generously and cannot be set with negative leading. If they were to be set solid (i.e. with zero leading) there's a strong possibility that a descender would clash with an ascender, causing an ugly scene within your running text.

Neutraface Slab Display

Humanist serif Centaur is split roughly into vertical thirds: ascender, x-height and descender.

CROSSBEAM
Furnace like heat
CONSTRUCT
Gridiron

MVB Solano Gothic, released between 2007 and 2010 by MVB Fonts, was originally designed for the city of Albany's signage system and feels suitably architectural and workmanlike, as though it's just turned up for a day's labour at the factory. MVB Solano Gothic includes a Retro style with a round topped 'A' and 'M' and it pairs neatly with Armada, a face inspired by nineteenth-century architecture designed by Tobias Frere-Jones in 1994.

On this page
Solano Gothic
Solano Gothic Retro
Armada

Turbine

Band Width

FACTORY

National Labour Relations

Take yourself back to the days of Bakelite radios powered by the output of massive turbines housed in monolithic brick and steel edifices. Radio, a very original Formal script from Village Constellation, comes in three 'band widths', AM, FM and SW, and recalls the atmosphere of those early technologies. Pairing with a unique Formal or Casual script like this can be tricky but Heron Sans' workplace aesthetic does the job perfectly well here.

On this page

Radio

Heron Sans

Heron Sans Condensed

Manufacture

Design & Build

Quality

Construction

Secure Fastenings

Grotesque sans Heron Sans made an appearance on the previous page and here we have its Grotesque Slab companion face, which is equally at home on the factory floor. Heron Serif, released by The Font Bureau in 2012, is even more capable of generating that feeling of humming industry with its equally weighted stems and serifs. Look at pairing it with the strong chiselled features of FF Scala to keep the industrial atmosphere going.

On this page

Heron Serif
Heron Serif Condensed
Scala
Scala Condensed

Salt Mine
Going Down
Pressure
Workshop

With names like Industry and Factoria, these companion fonts from Fort Foundry (Geometric sans Industry came first, followed by Geometric Slab Factoria, which is developed from Industry's glyph shapes) had to find their way into this section of the book. They both live up to their names very well, generating a strong visual sense of industry and effort. As connected faces they work together in perfect harmony.

On this page
Industry
Factoria

Trick #11 | Colour – the new black and white

To talk about typographic colour might initially make one think of a bold red headline or some evocatively tinted calligraphic script, but in fact the term has a rather more pragmatic meaning. It gets a mention on page 62 where we discuss contrast and actually refers to the overall tonal value, or visual weight, of a block or blocks of text. The best way to gauge typographic colour is to stare at a layout and adjust your focus (squinting at the printed surface or screen can help achieve this) so the text becomes slightly blurred. The grayscale tone that you see in place of the otherwise sharp text is the typographic colour.

Thinking about typeface choices that can provide typographic colour is another way to provide your text with any hierarchy that it might require. Contrasty typefaces can boost typographic colour, making it appear darker, as can weighty faces that feature heavy strokes. Lowercase glyphs are particularly important when gauging colour because their form is generally more variable than that of the corresponding uppercase glyphs with their consistent cap height. Your eye will naturally be drawn towards areas of a layout with a darker colour, and a variation in colour across different areas of layout helps to create a dynamic visual experience for the viewer.

We fade
to grey

Try the squint technique out on this page to see how typographic colour forms. Even though the lighter line of the above headline (set in Eames Century Modern Bold and Thin) is much larger than the running text these two areas are roughly equal in tone as the text is more dense, creating similar coverage.

BRAVE SERVICE

Uncompromising

Individuality

Shining example

A reputation for reliability and service is important, and Geometric sans serif Heroic Condensed from Type Trust is well able to perform in that specific area. Its added space-saving advantages as a specialist condensed face rather than a second-thought spin-off make it very versatile for all kinds of typographic applications. Pairing it with distinguished Humanist serif MVB Verdigris will ensure top marks from the Board of Directors.

On this page

Heroic Condensed
MVB Verdigris Big
MVB Verdigris

Brother
CAMARADERIE
Sister
WE ARE ONE...

FF Unit and FF Meta are both extended typeface families with numerous styles and are able to pair with either a close relative or a friendly neighbour. Both these faces are from FontFont of course – the clue is in their names – and they share width and form characteristics that allow them to be paired successfully with one another in many combinations. These are white-collar faces that are more comfortable in the office than on the factory floor.

On this page

FF Unit
FF Unit Slab
FF Meta
FF Meta Serif

FORD
TRANSIT BUSES

FIND WIDE ACCEPTANCE

Within little more than a year after their introduction, Ford Transit Buses have gained a recognized place in city transportation. More than a thousand have been delivered and are in full-time service. Twelve major American cities and many more smaller communities are now using them. Even cities in far-away countries have recognized their merits and purchased these buses. Their adoption is ever-increasing wherever modern passenger transportation is demanded.

Such wide and rapidly-increasing acceptance is noteworthy, for the purchase of transit buses depends almost entirely upon proof of economical operation—upon the ability to provide profitable returns from the investment in this form of transportation.

Ford Transit Buses have proved that they more than justify the investment in them. Their record of achievement is written in glowing testimonials. This testimony is founded not only upon years of experience in bus manufacture, but also upon more than three decades of automotive achievement in the field of low-cost transportation. The economy and profit-earning ability of Ford Transit Buses are therefore in keeping with Ford tradition.

Fleet of 12 Ford Transit Buses operated by Chicago Surface Lines

Client	Chicago Surface Lines
Studio/Designer	Unknown
Principal typefaces	Futura Display, Futura, Bodoni

The terrific graphic design created in support of industry during the earlier half of the twentieth century has never been bettered, as evidenced by this very contemporary-looking piece from 1939. Geometric sans Futura, designed twelve years earlier in 1927, was already demonstrating its enduring popularity which has lasted to the present day.

FUSE BOX
Electrickery
Nikola Tesla
Complex Circuit

DIN 1451 is the original 'technical' typeface developed in Germany in 1931 for use on all road signage, administrative and technical documentation. It's a Geometric sans serif with limited options – there are just two weights, the condensed Engschrift and medium-weight Mittelschrift. A direct variant of DIN 1451, Linotype's DIN Next (which followed the earlier improved variant FF DIN) provides greater flexibility through the addition of italics and further weights.

On this page
DIN 1451
DIN Next

Microchip

PowerPC

Über Geek

Cannot compute

GarageFont's Freight Micro has appeared several times in this book and has been described as both unusual and quirky. Its letterforms are certainly very individual, and I find them to be reminiscent of printed circuit boards. This is a prime example of personal interpretation – sometimes you don't need a rule to link a typeface to a theme, just a notion. The angularity of both Auto and Syntax forges visual connections with the versatile Freight Micro.

On this page

Freight Micro
Auto
Syntax

Kelvin

One moment in time

Ampere

Système International d'Unités

Forza, released by Hoefler & Co. in 2010, is a twenty-first-century Eurostile with some nifty nuances that bring it firmly up-to-date. The strokes taper noticeably where they meet the stems and this gives the face a technical air that it might well lack if it were not for this interesting innovation. Try it with another Geometric sans like Interstate with its angled terminals, or with a very understated Neo-Humanist sans like Unit.

On this page

Forza
Interstate
FF Unit

Electrical vehicle
Portability
SPEED FREAK
Limited range

FS Sinclair from Fontsmith wears its heart on its sleeve, declaring itself on Fontsmith's website as a technical type inspired by the inventor of the ZX Spectrum, Sir Clive Sinclair. The face works well as either a display or text face and its round forms, based on the flat-sided superellipse, visually connects with Hoefler and Co.'s Vitesse, a typeface faster than Sir Clive's less successful invention, the C5 electric car.

On this page
FS Sinclair
Vitesse

Ducting
Cable Television
BENT COPPER
Rewiring

ITC Conduit was designed by Mark van Bronkhorst in 1997 and is a slightly more rough and ready face than others featured in this technical theme. He based the letterforms on non-professional sign writing, using a fairly narrow grid and rounding corners as though they were formed by a pipe bender. The resulting face has a Postmodern feel to it and works with Humanist slab Adelle, a webfont favourite, or the oddly naïve letterforms of DIN Next Rounded.

On this page

ITC Conduit
Adelle
DIN Next Rounded

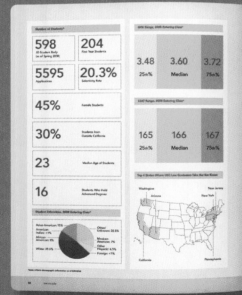

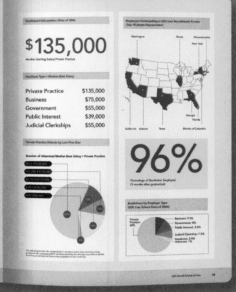

Client	USC Gould School of Law
Studio/Designer	AdamsMorioka/Sean Adams
Web	www.adamsmorioka.com
Principal typefaces	Century Expanded, Avenir

USC Gould School of Law asked AdamsMorioka to create a personal and approachable system to help increase applicant numbers and set them apart from similar institutions. Avenir introduces a slightly more humanist approach to its Geometric style, while Century Expanded fills the role of headline font on feature spreads.

Formal occasions demand formal typefaces and Bickham Script can certainly fill the role with aplomb. Richard Lipton's script was one of the first to capitalise on alternative glyph substitution techniques and you can spend hours trying out all the options available to embellish your typographic statement. The quiet neutrality of Transitional serif Centennial won't undermine Bickham Script's dominant presence, and Geometric sans Akkurat will intrude even less.

On this page

Bickham Script
Centennial
Akkurat

142

Single Malt

Smooth

Speyside Spirit

Dalwhinnie

A favourite lunchtime tipple

Conceived specifically for editorial use, TypeTogether's Abril references classic Didones alongside nineteenth-century Scotch Romans and Slabs. The titling and display weights are closest to the Didone style with their distinctively slim unbracketed serifs, but the text weights are closer to Transitional Scotch Romans with a form less like the titling weights than a first glance might imply, so be sure to use the correct weights in the right places.

On this page

Abril Display
Abril Titling
Abril Text

143

Silence

Introspective

Unspoken Truth

SERENELY RETICENT

The exquisite Humanist serif Requiem from Hoefler and Co. celebrates the beauty of handwriting with a four-style, eight-weight family of faces. Requiem Fine and Display take care of the larger setting requirements while the weightier Requiem Text is there for smaller point sizes. Geometric sans Verlag, also from Hoefler and Co., has a comparable x-height and its warmer qualities compared to other geometrics resist the chance to undermine the grace of Requiem.

On this page

Requiem
Verlag

Manuscript

Grammatical

CONSERVATIVE STRUCTURE

A characterful vocabulary

FF Yoga, released by FontFont in 2009, addresses the frustrations experienced by anyone that loves the feel of Gill Sans but has then tried to set it successfully in large quantities. The improvement in width consistency is the biggest advantage FF Yoga has over Gill Sans' idiosyncratic ways. Frills-free book face Joanna, an Eric Gill typeface from 1930 presenting fewer typographic challenges, works well when used as a pair with FF Yoga.

On this page

FF Yoga
Joanna MT

145

Nuptials

Mendelssohn

With this ring

I THEE WED

Formal occasions and typefaces that display an obvious level of penmanship go hand-in-hand, and Humanist serif Adobe Jenson is one of the best digital interpretations of a sixteenth-century serif. The lowercase 'e', with its distinctive beak, is a particularly attractive glyph that gives away the origins of the face instantly, and the large family contains a full range of optical variants. Try it with Hermann Zapf's Zapfino, a Formal script with a wealth of character and poise.

On this page

Adobe Jenson Display
Adobe Jenson
Zapfino Forte

An identity for a restaurant based around the theme of early nineteenth-century French brasseries. The font selection is large but carefully curated to create a cohesive turn-of-the-century mood for the various components.

Client	Keith McNally
Studio/Designer	Mucca Design/ Matteo Bologna, Victor Mingovits
Studio/Designer	mucca.com
Principal typefaces	Akzidenz Grotesk, Miehle, FF Bodoni Classic, Engravers MT, Americana, Modern No.20, Bickham Script, Bureau Grotesque

Principle #7 | Single- or double-storey?

Take a look at any number of typeface compendiums (including the excellent FontBook app for the iPhone and iPad by FontShop International) and you'll notice that the glyphs 'R', 'a' and 'g' are often used whenever a succinct visual sample needs to be displayed. These three glyphs tell you a lot about the design characteristics of a typeface – particularly in the case of the 'a' and 'g', which each come in two flavours, single- or double-storey. A 'g' can also be binocular when it's formed by a counter and ear in its upper portion, linked to a loop below the baseline.

The single-storey 'a' has proved to be relatively unpopular among typeface designers over the years and only makes an appearance in a few roman Geometric sans serif and Geometric slabs, and in Formal scripts. In part this is due to legibility issues; the single-storey 'a' is compromised because it can be confused with a lowercase 'o'. Despite this, a number of contemporary sans serif faces released in the OpenType format now contain an alternative single-storey glyph for the 'a'.

The double-storey 'a' provides a great method for checking whether a font is a genuine italic, or one that a designer has falsely skewed. Unlike roman weights, true italics always feature a single-storey 'a', so if you come across a slanted double-storey 'a' it's a sure sign that a bit of typographic cheating has been going on. Skewing type is a big no-no as it produces incorrect glyph shapes, so a proper italic weight should always be used; if you know you'll be needing an italic, make sure the typeface family you choose includes them.

The single-storey 'g' has been more successful; a decent portion of Geometric and Neo-Grotesque sans serif faces feature the single-storey glyph because the regular structure sits more comfortably with the design

Chronicle

ethos of these classifications. Outside of this group the 'g' appears almost exclusively in its double-storey form. Like the single-storey 'a', the single-storey 'g' is favoured for formal scripts as a more flexible linking letterform.

Double- and single-storey glyphs can work perfectly well together, and indeed appear together as standard glyphs in some typefaces, Helvetica being a well known example with its double-storey 'a' and single-storey 'g'. So why favour one over the other as part of a combination of typefaces? Single-storey characters are arguably more contemporary in appearance due to the regularity of their glyph shapes, so if you're looking to create a modern or technical feel, these two characters may well influence your choice.

Brown

Flash Gordon

Pulp Magazine

Ming the Merciless

Death Ray

Amazing Stories

Although Dynatype from Alphabet Soup certainly has a mid-twentieth-century hand-lettering vibe about it, for me it has something of the Flash Gordon or Buck Rogers vintage sci-fi going on too. It could be the association of sci-fi with comic books but it's not difficult to imagine the face emblazoned across Flash's tunic as he hunts down Ming the Merciless. Try pairing it with 1930s-inspired sans Brandon Text or the hi-tech FS Sinclair for some stylistic contrast.

On this page

Dynatype
Magda Clean
FS Sinclair

X-WING

Darth Vader

Great, Kid. Don't get cocky.

Chewbacca

The Empire

Hoefler & Co.'s monolithic display face Acropolis may be an historical revival based on nineteenth-century lettering styles but it could also look right at home set large across the side of a rocket ship blasting off for distant galaxies – it could almost be cut from plate steel. As a partner, the gently curving but otherwise sturdy Neo-Humanist sans Museo feels quite futuristic without obviously trying, and Avenir's relationship to Futura makes it an irresistible choice.

On this page

Acropolis
Museo
Avenir

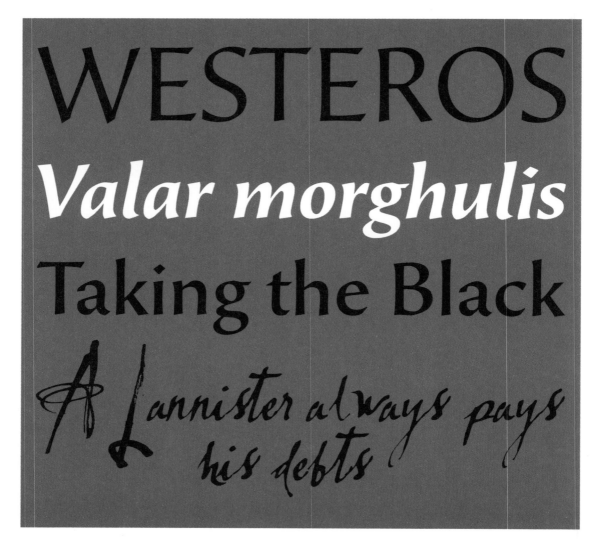

With swords and sorcery pre-eminent in everyone's favourite fantasy storylines, Humanist sans Beorcana from Terrestrial Design provides a wonderfully calligraphic option for both display and text setting. It's practically a script and looks as though it were handwritten with a broad-nibbed dip pen so it's perfect for magical lost-parchment typography. Sign off your story with Lassigue D'mato, a face that has a genuinely good stab at replicating scratchy handwriting.

On this page

Beorcana Display
Beorcana
Lassigue D'mato

152

Witchcraft

Scary Castle

Behind you!

The Accursed

Fantasy often involves a medieval-like setting so what better choice than a Blackletter face to evoke a sense of dark-age history? Fette Fraktur is almost the genuine article – it's not quite medieval but does date back to 1850 when it was designed by German punch cutter Johann Christian Bauer. The Contemporary Serif face Warnock is much newer, as is Humanist sans Cronos, but both these Adobe faces have a calligraphic air about them and pair well with the Blackletter form.

On this page

Fette Fraktur
Warnock
Cronos

Competitive Victory Take the Prize Go Team!

Neo-Humanist sans serif face Amplitude, released by Font Bureau in 2003, has some stand-out features that give it a lively character without sacrificing legibility or usefulness. It has a very large x-height and neat little nicks like the old-style ink traps found in cuts of metal type. Cholla Slab echoes some of that character with tapering where strokes meet vertical stems, and why not add in a flamboyant script like Studio Lettering Swing in case the cheerleaders arrive uninvited?

On this page

Amplitude
Cholla Slab
Studio Lettering Swing

Atlético
FOOTBALL
Team Strip
End to End
A Game of Two Halves

Vitesse is a Geometric slab from Hoefler & Co. that would look very comfortable on the back of a football shirt. It utilises a modified superellipse with slightly curving sides for its round letterforms, and feels extremely nimble at both large and small sizes. Gist Upright from Yellow Design Studio is an inline slab serif with a smattering of retro about it that works with, rather than against, the modernity of Vitesse, which has a close Geometric slab cousin in Quadon.

On this page

Vitesse
Gist Upright
Quadon

TEN PIN
Gutterball
STRIKE!
Perfect 300

Not all sport has to be aggressively competitive; there's a place for some lighthearted fun in any competition (apart from boxing perhaps), and Linotype's Inagur is a good typeface choice for spreading a little sporting camaraderie. I can't help thinking of a bowling pin whenever I look at the uppercase 'I'. For any straightforward setting required in this partnership, a Neo-Grotesque sans serif like Univers, with its single-storey 'g', will pair up well.

On this page

Inagur
Univers

VARSITY BLUES

Superbowl

The Rose Bowl, Pasadena

Gridiron

Princetown was originally released by Letraset back in 1981 and takes its inspiration from the distinctive Geometric sans outline faces seen frequently on American college sportswear. It's clearly a display face and has no lowercase characters, so a Geometric slab like Rockwell can be successfully substituted in for any additional text setting. Alternatively, Neo-Humanist sans serif TheMix from LucasFonts provides a vibrant partner without the Slab serif details.

On this page
PRINCETOWN
Rockwell
TheMix

Metroscript from Michael Doret's Alphabet Soup Foundry oozes American sporting atmosphere – it screams baseball and feels right at home sitting on the bleachers at Yankee Stadium. Always use the metrics option when setting Metroscript because the character pairs won't work correctly otherwise. Brandon Text, with its slightly rounded corners for that vintage look, or the classic Grotesque slab Clarendon, make comfortable bedfellows.

On this page

Metroscript
Brandon Grotesque
Clarendon

Client	The Eephus League / personal project
Studio/Designer	Bethany Heck
Web	heckhouse.com
Principal typefaces	Hercules, Sweet Sans, Herald Gothic, United Sans, Champion Gothic

The Eephus League, an ongoing personal project begun whilst Bethany Heck was a student, references the rich visual history of baseball through the use of carefully selected typefaces alongside vintage imagery. The 'eephus' is a slow pitch designed to fool the batter into hitting a strike.

Principle #8 | Serif shapes and bracketing

Serif letterforms have been with us since Roman times, appearing in Latin inscriptions carved into stone. There are a number of possible explanations for their introduction, including the theory that they were devised to clean up the ends of the principle strokes of glyphs prior to the completion of the carving. Serifs come in three main flavours: *hairline*, *slab* (or square) and *wedge*, and are further defined as either *bracketed* or *unbracketed*.

Hairline serifs are easy to spot; the description indicates that they're considerably thinner than the main strokes of the glyph. They're a prominent feature of Modern (or Didone) serifs such as the familiar and widely used Didot and Bodoni. Slab serifs are squared with 90-degree corners and can be as heavy or even heavier than a glyph's other strokes. When the serifs of a slab serif become thicker than its strokes, the stress characteristics of the typeface switch from vertical to horizontal (see also page 20). **Clarendon** and **Rockwell** are typical examples of (respectively) Grotesque and Geometric slab serifs. Wedge serifs are triangular and can arguably be described as a relatively modern innovation in terms of printed (but not inscribed) type. Their sharp character mimics that of a glyph engraved into stone or metal rather more than one created with a pen, and in recent years a number of fine typefaces featuring prominent wedge serifs have been released, including **Farnham** and **Neue Swift**.

Serifs can be either bracketed or unbracketed. A bracketed serif transitions in a smooth curve at the point where it joins a stroke, while an unbracketed serif joins the stroke abruptly, often at a right angle. Fifteenth-century Humanist typefaces tend to feature bracketed serifs with a fairly organic curve, reflecting the relatively primitive nature of the printing technology available at the time. As the quality of ink and paper improved, so did the sharpness and detail of serifs; Transitional typefaces feature finer bracketing with more precise curves. Today's digital technology means just about anything is possible, and Contemporary serifs take their influences from any and all preceding classifications, the side effect of this being that many such faces are difficult to classify.

When using serif shapes as a signpost to a successful typeface combination, think about mood as well as context and practical requirements. Blunt organic serifs work well when used to conjure up a sense of history while sharp wedges can generate energy and give your type a cutting-edge feel with a touch of traditional elegance thrown in for good measure.

Serif

Early humanist serifs like those which Adobe Jenson is based on were organically imprecise compared to later serif shapes, reflecting their calligraphic origins.

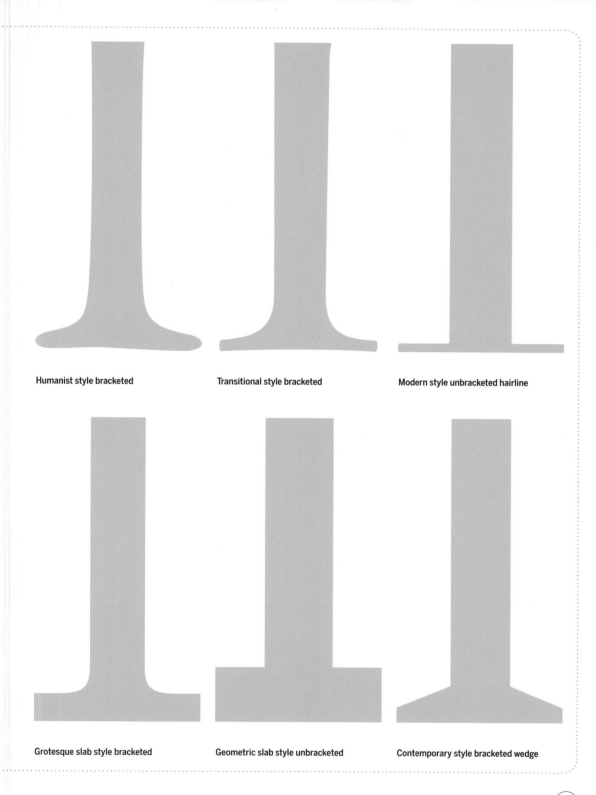

Humanist style bracketed

Transitional style bracketed

Modern style unbracketed hairline

Grotesque slab style bracketed

Geometric slab style unbracketed

Contemporary style bracketed wedge

WORLDLY
CHIC
EVOLVED
Cosmopolitan
Enlightened

Hoefler and Co.'s Idlewild is a bit of a chameleon. It can look sophisticated and straightforward at the same time and blend in or jump out as required. Much of its character on the page is governed by the weight selection, for which there are five choices, and it works beautifully with HTF Didot when sophistication is part of the brief. Monotype's Humanist serif Bembo Book works well as an accompanying text face.

On this page

IDLEWILD
HTF Didot
Bembo Book MT

The Sun King

LOUIS XIV

Monarch of the House of Bourbon

The incredibly beautiful SangBleu from Swiss Typefaces is based on an eighteenth-century French typeface known as Romain du Roi. It was commissioned by Louis XIV for exclusive use by the official printing works of the French Government and first appeared in 1702. Its contemporary counterpart is the epitome of sophistication in every regard and demands a gentle accompaniment for smaller text setting, so try a delicate Humanist sans like Cronos.

On this page

SangBleu
SangBleu Sans
Cronos

Alluring

Charisma & Style

Elegant beauty

Decent men prefer intelligence

Ingeborg, a 2009 face by Michael Hochleitner for Typejockeys, is a popular choice for glamorous but tasteful display setting. The Fat Italic weight is particularly pleasing to the eye when set at larger sizes, and the face is equally successful when used for text as it manages to retain its sense of glamour at smaller point sizes. Try it with FF Dax if you need a less expressive face for captions or footnotes.

On this page

Ingeborg
FF Dax

A quiet *Stunner* that takes some handling

Brandon Grotesque from HVD Fonts has a warmth to it despite its Geometric sans letterforms, which might otherwise be more clinical. Close inspection reveals that the corners of the evenly weighted strokes are slightly blunted, giving the face a softer look when set at larger point sizes. Its understated sophistication can provide a calming influence when flamboyant scripts like Erotica enter the equation.

On this page
Brandon Grotesque
Erotica

Civilized
ELEGANCE
urbanity
Poise & Finesse
Savoir Faire

Linotype's Glyphic serif face Meridien has been around since 1957 when Adrian Frutiger designed it for Deberny & Peignot. It has a fairly large x-height, which makes for a highly legible typeface, and the finely pointed serifs with their moderately cupped terminals create an air of sharp sophistication, as does Fontsmith's FS Clerkenwell, which is relatively narrow for a Grotesque slab. The lighter weights work surprisingly well within this theme.

On this page

Meridien
FS Clerkenwell

Client	Sankeys
Studio/Designer	Yolo/Martin Fewell
Web	www.yolo.info
Principal typefaces	ITC Caslon 224, Carousel

Yolo has designed posters for Sankeys nightclub since 2006. This poster, worked cleverly around the theme of the number 9, creates a sense of sophistication around a potentially riotous club event.

SWANKY
BLING
$1,500
Luxury Purchase
Deep Pockets

Luxury Diamond is every designer label rolled into one. When it was first released by designers Christian Schwartz and Dino Sanchez it had a spoof price tag of $1,500 to emphasise its opulent allure, and it wouldn't look out of place on any luxury product as long as there was enough width to set the required word. Text setting is obviously out of the question so try a Didone like Bauer Bodoni or a Gothic sans like Griffith Gothic alongside this preening exhibitionist of a typeface.

On this page

LUXURY DIAMOND
Bauer Bodoni
Griffith Gothic

Sumptuous Luxury

Grandiose

Stay at *The Ritz*

Exhaust a lavish budget

Like Luxury Diamond on the opposite page, Lust Script by Positype demands attention and space and comes into its own when set at large point sizes. The script style is even more sumptuous than the Modern serifs that make up the rest of this family and it pairs rather well with various cuts of Caslon. Try ITC Caslon 224 for larger (although not too large) headlines but switch to Adobe Caslon for smaller text setting.

On this page

Lust Script Display

Lust Display Didone

ITC Caslon 224

Adobe Caslon

When you first start to use Maximiliano Sproviero's extraordinary Erotica script it can be a daunting experience because there are so many options for alternative flourishes and linking characters. However, as you get to know which flourishes work best at the beginning or end of a word, and with which individual characters, things begin to get a little easier. Use the typeface as large as possible; anything below 48 point begins to look too cramped and uncomfortable.

On this page

Archer

Trick #12 | Ligatures

EAT ALE ASP

 Ligatures on

Ligatures off

EAT ALE ASP

The OpenType format's ability to accommodate a large number of individual glyphs (up to a staggering 65,536) and its advanced layout features, which include the automatic replacement of sequential characters with a ligature or an alternative single glyph, has increased our ability to control the appearance of text enormously. In the above illustration, with text set in the Display face **Ed Interlock** and in uppercase, the dramatic effect produced by switching ligatures on can be seen clearly. In this example the cap 'A' interacts with its neighbours in three different ways depending on which glyphs it falls between. Additionally the 'T', 'L' and 'S' switch contextually as each word is set – typographic magic! A single glyph can now represent multiple characters (i.e. an ff or fi ligature) and, depending on which settings governing OpenType behaviour are checked, your layout application will automatically select the appropriate alternative ligature as you type. **Ed Interlock** is admittedly an extreme example of OpenType ligatures in action and serves us well

for this example, but all OpenType typefaces offer this high degree of controllability, limited only by the number of individual glyphs included in the package.

Ed Interlock contains over 1,400 separate ligatures!

Some conventional ligatures from Bauer Bodoni, Futura ND, Neue Swift and Neutraface Slab Text.

Berlin
Sally Bowles
A musical extravaganza
Kit Kat Club

Saracen from Hoefler and Co. is a Glyphic serif based loosely on nineteenth-century display styles, yet it feels rather more contemporary because of its relatively straightforward proportions. In its day the face would likely have featured a wider body but this design is far more useful and therefore flexible. It pairs really well with the extensive Knockout family, especially when used on posters where both faces can be set at fairly large point sizes.

On this page

Saracen
Knockout

Client	TIPI AM KANZLERAMT
Studio/Designer	upstruct
Studio/Designer	www.upstruct.com
Principal typefaces	Saracen, Knockout

TIPI AM KANZLERAMT is a marquee theatre based in Berlin which brings to life the variety performances of the 1920s. Saracen and Knockout are both typefaces with enough presence and personality to match the flamboyant character of this famous production.

Liza is a live-script typeface designed by Underware, meaning it dynamically selects the best alternate characters from its collection of over 4,000 glyphs as you type, thus closely replicating genuine handwritten script. There are three styles in the family, display, text and caps, plus a font made up of pretty ornaments and decorations. Adobe's Humanist serif Brioso, with its prominently calligraphic form, pairs well for text setting.

On this page

Liza Display

Brioso

Core Circus from S-Core comprises twenty different styles that can be overlaid to create precisely aligned settings composed of different elements including dots, fine inline rules, drop shadows and outlines. It's clearly intended for display use alone, and complex effects can be achieved very quickly and easily. Using a playful script like Sign Painter House Upright will conjure up that circus handbill feeling, and a chunky Grotesque slab like Giza will add to the fun.

On this page

CORE CIRCUS

SIGN PAINTER HOUSE UPRIGHT

Giza

Crafted cheer
Good Times
J'amuse
at all times

Eames Century Modern was designed by Erik van Blokland for House Industries and is a great choice of face for projects that require a degree of humorous abandon without losing all sense of decorum. It's bursting with character but well-crafted at the same time and is flexible enough to work at both display and text sizes. Pairing it with a good quality Casual script like The Carpenter from Fenotype can heighten the sense of retro that imbues this Grotesque slab.

On this page

Eames Century Modern
The Carpenter

Alfredo
e Toto
Projectionist
The Golden Age

Kinescope by Mark Simonson recalls a golden age of cinema when hand-lettered scripts appeared regularly in film titles, and brush and pen lettering was the only way one could achieve type that looked like this. It's another face built around OpenType technology and succeeds where so many previous attempts at a realistic script fail. Try using a Geometric sans serif like Futura ND or a Modern serif like Abril to retain that mid-century flavour.

On this page

Kinescope
Futura ND
Abril Titling

FS Olivia from Fontsmith is an unusual Contemporary serif with a lot of penmanship built into its interestingly irregular letterforms. Calligraphic strokes combine with straight-edged counters that might have come from a Glyphic serif carved in stone. Fenotype's Alek is a jolly Casual script that works well with a serif like FS Olivia, and Monotype's Walbaum adds a slightly more historical tone while keeping things light and airy.

On this page

FS Olivia

Alek

Walbaum MT

P. G. WODEHOUSE

SUMMER LIGHTNING

Client	Everyman
Designer/Illustrator	Peter B. Willberg/Andrzej Klimowski
Web	pbwillberg.com
Principal typefaces	New Yorker Type, ITC Franklin Gothic

The wonderful P. G. Wodehouse series published by Everyman features a consistent cover styling that uses two typefaces synonymous with the author's early years in America.

Principle #9 | **Which script?**

Scripts are derived from the cursive strokes of handwritten text or lettering. They began to appear sporadically as fonts in the late eighteenth century and are traditionally split into two categories, Formal and Casual, but I subscribe to a system that incorporates a third category, Calligraphic, as it provides a home for certain styles that fall somewhere between the other two.

Formal scripts are based on the fine writing styles of the seventeenth and eighteenth centuries where letterforms were drawn with a metal-nib dip pen. Pens of this type are able to produce a modulated stroke by varying the pressure applied to the pointed nib, thus forcing the tines to spread apart, so many formal scripts feature contrasting strokes with a forwards-leaning stress.

Casual scripts, as the term implies, disregard the formalities of fine handwriting and transmit a more emancipated aesthetic – think of a market trader's marker-penned price tags or vintage sign writing. The style first appeared during the early half of the twentieth century and was popularised by advertising art directors and by lettering artists working on the hugely popular pulp magazines of the 1920s and 1930s. They remain in favour for any application that requires a sense of fun, historical vernacular or irreverence.

Calligraphic is a useful term to apply to any scripts that are difficult to specifically label as either Formal or Casual. Typefaces can include any that emulate traditional broad-nib calligraphy with moderate to high stroke contrast, or those that attempt to replicate informal handwriting. A prime candidate for inclusion in this category is *Suomi Hand Script*, a particularly successful OpenType font that emulates natural handwriting extremely well. Yes, it's a casual script, but if you're rooting through your typeface collection for a handwriting style face, it's helpful to narrow things down.

The list of potential uses and combination opportunities for scripts is long and they are very much in vogue at the time of writing. Not so long ago, working with script faces was not a particularly rewarding task and the best way to achieve a convincing result was to commission a lettering artist and avoid typesetting altogether. However, the advent of OpenType, with multiple glyphs and contextual alternatives, has changed things completely and nowadays the best script faces can be set with relative ease. Remember to select the 'Standard Ligature' and 'Contextual Alternates' settings in software such as InDesign and always use 'Metrics' rather than 'Optical' kerning to keep the text flowing smoothly.

Script faces released in the OpenType format generally provide a choice of glyphs with alternative swashes and links.

Here we have (from top to bottom) samples of a Formal script, a Casual script and a Calligraphic script; Bickham Script, The Carpenter and Suomi Hand Script. Note that the Calligraphic script is designed to work at smaller point sizes and is less convincing at 200 point, the size at which these examples have been set.

Chuckle

Comic Turn

Rib Tickler

Light-hearted jocularity

If you choose a novelty typeface in an attempt to portray humour it's simply going to fight with any humorous content and will probably look bad anyway. However, typefaces with a cheery air about them are useful in this context and Doko certainly fits the bill. This Contemporary Humanist serif from Urdt is extremely lighthearted and with its large x-height it pairs nicely with a sans serif like Pimlico, a Humanist face from Fontsmith.

On this page

Doko
Pimlico

L.O.L.
Split my sides
Crack me up
You've got me in stitches!
Rolling in the aisles

Farao, a Grotesque slab from Storm, never fails to put a smile on my face when I see it. It's a fully realised typeface family with a range of optical text weights but works brilliantly as headline text with an ability to infuse any setting with a sense of fun. Abril Text can also do this – the curled details on lowercase hooks and terminals function similarly to Farao's, and FF Balance's reverse contrast and open honesty add to the sense of fun.

On this page

Farao
Abril Text
FF Balance

Smile

Happy Face

Jollification

Come On Get Happy

Bree, a Humanist display sans from TypeTogether, is type with a smile on its face, especially if the lowercase 'e' is involved. Other touches, like the looped 'k' and 'g', support the cheerfulness of this face and it's very popular with web designers. FF Dax is similarly cheery, despite its Neo-Humanist sans classification due to the organic nature of the letterforms, but try FF Daxline for text since it offers improved options with its lower contrast and more consistent character widths.

On this page
Bree
FF Dax
FF Daxline

Rejigging

Frutiger

Rejigging

Johnston

Rejigging

Fedra Sans and Fedra Sans Alt

A *tittle* is the term used to describe the small diacritic marks (e.g. an accent or an umlaut) that appear above glyphs that require specific pronunciation when spoken, as well as the dot (ovoid or square) above the lowercase 'i' and 'j'. When set as running text, the shape and size of a typeface's tittles are less noticeable to the untrained eye, but when text is set at larger sizes, the shape and position of the tittles become visually more prominent and their character can help to inject personality. Note that many specialist display typefaces feature square tittles; the larger surface area (compared to a dot) aids legibility at a distance, a prime example being **Frutiger**, commissioned in 1968 for France's newly built Charles de Gaulle International Airport.

It's surprising how unique a typeface can look simply by rotating a square tittle through 45-degrees, as evidenced by **Underground** (or **Johnston**), the famous London Underground typeface designed by Edward Johnston in 1916. A number of typefaces, for example **Fedra Sans**, which also features those diamond-shaped tittles, contain alternative glyphs for the lowercase 'i' and 'j' with tittles of differing shapes or orientations more suited

to running text set at smaller point sizes. If you ever need to set a typeface intended primarily for use as running text at larger sizes and it doesn't contain alternative display glyphs or weights, consider outlining the characters and nudging the tittles down slightly so they're closer to the x-height line. Tittles can sometimes appear to be too high on the body in glyphs that aren't designed specifically for display use.

Freehand

For your amusement

Badinage

Wisecrack

Dynascript from Alphabet Soup is another OpenType triumph from Michael Doret, one of the original innovators of Casual script typefaces for the digital age. It's a fun-infused typeface reminiscent of Speedball lettering from the 1930s–40s and can't fail to brighten up any layout that can accept its retro looks. The brushwriting inspiration behind FS Pimlico means it pairs well with Dynascript, and the face offers eight weights for text and headline setting.

On this page

Dynascript
FS Pimlico

Client	Hardie Grant Publishing
Studio/Designer	Luke Lucas
Web	lukelucas.com
Principal typefaces	Ed Interlock, Ed Gothic, Cincinnati Poster

A book about hilarious visions of the future from the past demands a certain look, partly achieved by the illustration style but also ably supported by the choice of a bevy of retro style typefaces.

CEREAL BOX
Word Balloon
PULP FICTION
Eat your greens!

Ed Benguiat is a veteran typographer, known particularly for his lettering styles, who collaborated with House Industries to release the Ed Benguiat collection in 2004. It comprises six individual styles: three display faces, two Casual scripts and a set of dingbats (or Bengbats in this case). Any or all can be worked together in a layout to produce a comic-book effect with the amazing Ed Interlock taking the prize for most innovative use of OpenType ligatures.

On this page
Ed Interlock
Ed Brush
Ed Gothic

Fedora is actually quite a cheesy typeface that seems to be available as a free download just about everywhere. This should put you off because free font websites should generally be avoided, but somehow this one works for me. The outline version is the best style: it's very *Raiders of the Lost Ark* meets *Boy's Own* comic book. Try pairing it with a face like Amasis, which twins the solid feel of a Slab serif with a Humanist serif to create a characterful face for headlines and text.

On this page

FEDORA

Amasis

COUNTERCULTURE
Suitable for adults
ALTERNATIVE HUMOUR
MAIL ORDER OFFERS
IRREVERENCE!

House Industries is well known as a source of quality hand-lettered script typefaces that never quite stray into the no-mans-land of the 'novelty' font, although a few admittedly walk a fine line. Fink Sans is part of the eight-style family known as Rat Fink and has comic-book headline written all over it. Try it with a Geometric sans like MVB Solano Gothic, which can channel a complementary retro feel that pairs well with Casual scripts.

On this page

FINK SANS
MVB Solano Gothic

Pique from Process Type Foundry creates quite a buzz wherever it appears. It's a Casual script based closely on the strokes of a brush marker – there's a lot about this face that reminds one of traditional sign writing but also of graffiti tags, which is where the comic-book connection comes in. It needs to be paired with a cheerful and open-minded face with Humanist leanings, so try something like TypeTogether's Pollen (for text) or Bree (for legible headline setting).

On this page

Pique

Pollen

Bree

Convincing penmanship

Swatch

Scribble and Scrawl

Straightforward legibility

The majority of typefaces that attempt to recreate realistic handwriting fail to do so for a variety of reasons. They usually look too uniform or rigid, with lots of unnatural links between character pairs, but this isn't the case with Suomi Hand Script. Once again, the magic of OpenType organises hundreds of ligatures and character pairs into a convincing order. Try pairing it with a clean Geometric sans like Urban Grotesk to offset its handwritten texture.

On this page

Suomi Hand Script
Urban Grotesk

ROUGHLY RENDERED

TWANG!

KEEP OFF THE CONCRETE

Polite Notice

House Movements Poster is part of another collection of hand-drawn lettering faces from House Industries that goes under the collective name of Movements. Personally, I think it's the best of the five fonts in the package in terms of its natural-looking letterforms; characters appear to have been daubed onto a wall with a fat, round-ended signwriter's brush. Once again, try pairing it with a low-profile face with clean lines such as News Gothic.

On this page

HOUSE MOVEMENTS POSTER

News Gothic

The Carpenter, released by Fenotype in 2014, is a highly versatile Casual script with a wealth of OpenType features accessed via the OpenType menu of your chosen software. There are the usual swashes, contextual and stylistic alternate glyphs and a set of three ornament and pictogram styles accompanying the three weights. It's a particularly lively script, which pairs well with other well-sculpted faces such as Monotype's Contemporary serif Alisal.

On this page

The Carpenter
Alisal

The letterforms of Lassigue D'mato are highly illustrative and not that easy to read so this typeface is best used for setting an historical scene with a few short words dropped in before or after more conventional running text. The range of available glyphs is relatively limited in comparison to some other OpenType offerings – there are 212 – but this is enough to achieve a result. To continue the historical theme, try a classic Humanist serif like Adobe Jenson.

On this page

Lassigue D'mato
Adobe Jenson

ROME
Marcus Aurelius
27 B.C. – A.D. 395
The United Empire

Glyphic serif Trajan is a go-to typeface for anything needing a grand announcement or a dramatic entrance. Released by Adobe as one of its earliest digital fonts in 1989, it's suffered from overuse over the years but undeniably manages to recapture the grace of its inspiration, the characters carved into the base of Trajan's Column in Rome. Goudy Old Style subs in well, given the lack of Trajan text weights, and Syntax's Humanist qualities provide a sans serif partner.

On this page

TRAJAN
Goudy Old Style
Syntax

American Art

Retrospective

The Collection

Rights Managed

Referencing sobriety

Hoefler & Co.'s Gothic sans Whitney was originally developed for New York's Whitney Museum and works well both as text and as a signage face. It's particularly useful for annotating infographics since an extensive range of 'indexing' glyphs are present, and its narrow width saves space. Chronicle Text shares its width characteristics and a similar x-height means it pairs well. Melior is a more unusual fit but will nonetheless add gravitas to text of a serious nature.

On this page

Whitney
Chronicle Text
Melior

Cool
Research
DISSERTATION
Late-night study period
Detailed footnotes

Hoefler & Co.'s Verlag was created for the Guggenheim Museum but has subsequently been expanded to five weights with accompanying italics and three separate widths. Echoes of Futura are present in this twenty-first-century realisation of a pre-war Geometric sans but any historical niggles have been ironed out. Its relatively low x-height and narrow body harmonise well with Warnock, Adobe's large Contemporary serif family that includes four optical sizes.

On this page

Verlag
Warnock

Theory
Extensive research
Six-part documentary
Spin-off publishing deal

Arnhem, an OurType face released in 2001, is first and foremost a hardworking newspaper typeface but it's also an attractive Transitional serif with a high contrast that creates strong colour on the page. It also has an unusually large x-height, which helps it to hold its own against a broad range of sans serif faces. Try it with Section from Luxtypo, a Neo-Humanist sans with a potent authority about it that would lend itself to scientific papers or complex dissertations.

On this page

Arnhem Display
Arnhem
Section

Dictionary
Space saving
123 456
Lining or non-lining
Magnifying

Lexicon hails from Dutch foundry Enschedé and was created specifically for use in dictionaries. It's designed to generate maximum readability when space is at a premium yet it manages to do this without sacrificing any of the character one would associate with a good Transitional serif. There are a total of six weights with accompanying italics in two styles: Lexicon No.1 with short extenders, and Lexicon No.2 (with longer extenders) that can be set with increased leading.

On this page

Lexicon No.1
Lexicon No.2

2013 HOUSTON SYMPHONY BALL

RUSSIAN
Rhapsody

a **WHITE NIGHT** salute to
Hans & Margarita Graf

PHOEBE AND BOBBY TUDOR, CHAIRMEN

Honoring
MAESTRO HANS GRAF & MARGARITA GRAF
Community Partner Honoree
RICE UNIVERSITY

Client	Houston Symphony
Studio/Designer	CORE Design Studio
Web	coredesignstudio.com
Principal typefaces	Trajan, Almibar Pro, Fedra Sans, Odile

Branding and identity work for a prestigious annual event, the Houston Symphony Ball, using a typeface combination which portrays both seriousness and flamboyance.

Principle #10 | **Pen or chisel?**

With the exception of Geometric sans serif typefaces, which don't have noticeably variable stroke widths, contrast and serif shape can strongly influence typeface choices. Both these features help to indicate whether a typeface is derived in part from historical letterforms that were created on paper with either a pen or a brush, carved into stone, or engraved onto a metallic surface.

Typefaces derived from pen-drawn letterforms are discussed throughout the book so let's focus on Glyphic typefaces for a moment. Imagine the difference between drawing a character on a soft paper surface, then trying to create the same shapes by chiselling into a hard stone surface, and you'll get a feel for the harder-edged features of a Glyphic face. The first significant feature to look out for is the way strokes, legs and tails end with a flare instead of a serif or a blunt terminal. That's not to say that Glyphics never have serifs because many do, but they're usually small wedge-shaped serifs. A notable exception is TRAJAN, which features long tapered serifs but is nonetheless a Glyphic with a design based on the inscription at the base of Trajan's Column in Rome. The flaring and/or serifs are both references to the natural details that result from the chiselling process, where the craftsperson is attempting to keep corners as clean and sharp as possible. Running the chisel out of a grooved stroke into a flare or small wedged serif helps to achieve this in practice.

Trajan

Second, the shapes of Glyphic apertures, counters or loops may feature one or more flat sides that adjoin strokes at an angle rather than as a progressive curve – **Albertus** provides us with a fine example of this. When drawing glyphs with a pen, the negative spaces within are formed simultaneously by the strokes, but a carved glyph has its counters and apertures cut from within the shape of the letterform, so the process is somewhat different and straight lines are simpler to follow.

If you're looking for a typeface that provides a feeling of solidity or tradition, a Glyphic face can be the right choice. The association of the letterforms with the permanency of carved stone or engraved metal creates the sense that Glyphic faces can be relied on and trusted.

Albertus

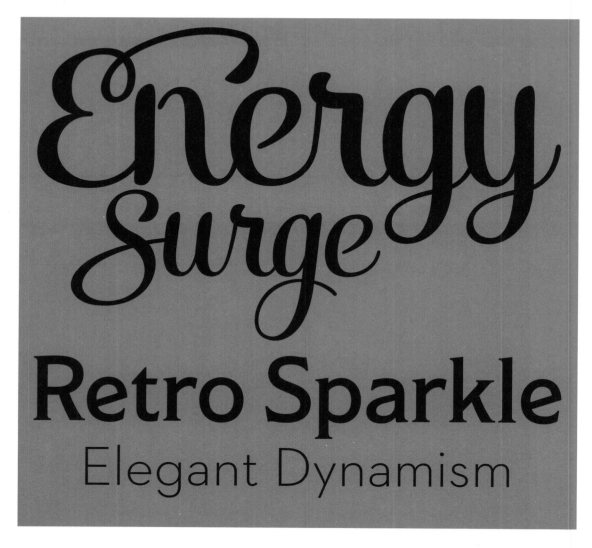

Alek is fun to look at and it's fun to use too. This upright Casual script from Fenotype comprises two weights with accompanying italics, which is uncommon for a script, plus an ornaments font for extra embellishments. It's also fully equipped to take advantage of OpenType functionality. A cool face with a retro vibe such as Modesto won't be overwhelmed by Alek's personality, while the elegance of Neutraface 2 belies its ability to look rather vivacious.

On this page

Alek

Modesto

Neutraface 2 Text

Party!

Carry 3 bottles

Eccentric
Guest List

BRING A BEAUTIFUL FRIEND

FS Lola from Fontsmith is an enthusiastic typeface that grabs you by the arm and drags you along to the party. Its terminals and tails are littered with cheeky little curves that look as though they're about to tickle adjacent characters, and the italic weights have a single-storey 'g' and 'y' with cheerful closed loops. Try it alongside Transitional serif Farnham, which is full of vibrant energy and endowed with a wealth of eccentricities.

On this page

FS Lola
Farnham

POW!

Luminesce

Glowworm

Soft-bodied beetle

The vibrancy of FS Pimlico from Fontsmith lies in its Humanist geometry inspired by brushwriting, a form that is particularly evident in the heaviest of the three available weights, which all come with an italic, and in Pimlico Glow with its hinted details. At home with everything from small text setting to display and signage, pair it with something unusual like Humanist Slab Freight Text.

On this page

Pimlico Glow

Pimlico

Freight Text

Effervesce

A fun slab to be with

Sharp cocktails

Let's have a nightcap?

Farao fizzes with humour and energy and manages to generate a level of jollity that other Clarendon style Grotesque Slabs fail to achieve. Not that they necessarily should, but having a typeface choice that can do this while still referencing its nineteenth-century ancestry could be just what you need. A lively serif like Contemporary Neue Swift, with its large x-height and spiky wedge-shaped serifs, will partner well.

On this page

Farao
Neue Swift

Trick #14 | Fractious fractions

This is the true glyph for the fraction as it appears in the character set of Adelle Extra Bold.

It's true that you'll not need to allow for the typesetting of fractions for every layout you undertake but it's so much better to set fractions correctly: ¼ rather than 1/4, or literally setting 0.25 which arguably looks worse in running text since you read it as 'point two five' rather than 'a quarter'. Most fonts, whether they're Postscript or OpenType, will contain at least a few dedicated fraction glyphs – commonly ¼, ½ and ¾. However, many OpenType fonts now contain several more to provide better options for specialist projects involving a lot of numerical information. For example, **Adelle**, which has proved to be a very popular choice for web designers, contains glyphs for ¼, ⅓, ½ and ¾, plus ⅔, ⅖, ⅗, ⅘, ⅙, ⅚, ⅐, ²⁄₇, ³⁄₇, ⁴⁄₇, ⁵⁄₇, ⁶⁄₇, ⅛, ⅜, ⅝, ⅞, ⅑, ²⁄₉, ⁴⁄₉, ⁷⁄₉ and ⁸⁄₉. If you know you're going to need a lot of fractions, take the glyph availability into account when making your typeface choices because special substitute glyphs are by far the best option.

As an aside, any combination of numbers separated by a slash can be turned into a fraction using a combination of size, baseline shift and kerning, but take care. If anyone apart from you is likely to work on your documents (e.g. in a professional publishing environment) ensure that you're all using the same conversion method, otherwise fractions created by different people won't match throughout the layout.

This fraction has been created with a script which resizes the numerator and denominator – it looks very different to the genuine glyph designed by Veronika Burian and José Scaglione.

In this version the fraction hasn't received any special formatting. It's visually acceptable at this point size but wouldn't look right in running text.

Aniuk, a display face with a robust and adventurous personality, and Bree, a display face that can actually be used at fairly small sizes (but not really for running text) practically recite the words out loud. The form of both these faces is quite similar but the ability to set Bree smaller could make for a useful pairing. Brandon Text is a much quieter fellow but its open apertures and clean curves make it a decent choice here for any accompanying text.

On this page

Aniuk
Bree
Brandon Text

Core Magic from S-Core is another of those clever layered typefaces that are appearing on a regular basis nowadays. Twenty alternative styles make up the complete family, and any and all can be duplicated one above the other to form 'multi-glyphs' that align perfectly and allow different colours or tints to be applied to each layer. It's not suitable for text of course, but Hoefler & Co.'s Sentinel is, it being one of the few Clarendons that come with real italic weights.

On this page

CORE MAGIC
Sentinel

GUM OF THE AMERICAS

CHICLE

ANCIENT MAYA TO WILLIAM WRIGLEY

NIFER P. MATHEWS

THE CHEWING GUM OF THE AMERICAS

CHICLE

FROM THE ANCIENT MAYA TO WILLIAM WRIGLEY

JENNIFER P. MATHEWS

E AMERICAS

LE E

WILLIAM WRIGLEY

HEWS

EWING GUM OF

CHIC

ANCIENT MAYA TO

JENNIFER P. M

Client	University of Arizona Press
Studio/Designer	Salamander Hill Design/David Drummond
Web	www.salamanderhill.com
Principal typefaces	Copperplate Gothic, Frutiger

A suitably vibrant cover for this book which tells the story of chicle, the sticky white extract of the Mesoamerican sapodilla tree. The characteristic small, sharp serifs of Glyphic Copperplate Gothic work nicely with the angular elements of the illustration.

William Wordsworth

Poetic licence

A breath of fresh air

Flora and Fauna

Fresh cut grass

Pollen from TypeTogether is poetry on the page, a gentle stroll by a meandering river on a beautiful summer's day. If you're lucky you may even spot a host of golden daffodils! It's a Contemporary serif with very large apertures to let all that fresh air in, and its calligraphic influence is worn proudly on its ruffled sleeve. A formal chaperon might be a good idea here, so try something from the Thesis collection, either TheSerif or TheSans set in an extra light weight.

On this page

Pollen
TheSerif
TheSans

Flight

Above the clouds

Sunshine and showers

What a lovely view

Flirt Script from Positype consists of two styles, Display and Regular, and both are as light as a feather. The face is extremely youthful in character and mimics a natural flowing style that can't fail to beguile any passing romantic with a poem in his head and flower in his buttonhole. If the requirement for small accompanying text isn't too demanding, say just a couple of stanzas, the pretty typeface Cronos may be all you need.

On this page

Flirt Display
Flirt Regular
Cronos

BASILICA

NAVE AND TRANSEPT

SUNDAY SERVICE

CLOISTER

Sanctuary

Hoefler & Co.'s Topaz, with its quiet Glyphic qualities, conjures up images of hushed cloisters and leafy churchyards. Its regular style can be visually split into two using a pair of layered alternatives, giving you the option to apply a different colour to the characters and their inline detail. The engraved letterforms of Copperplate Gothic are equally serene, with their tiny, sharp corner flicks, and Humanist serif Cala provides the necessary calmness of form for text setting.

On this page

TOPAZ
COPPERPLATE GOTHIC
Cala

NOVEL
Manuscript
Hardback
Paperback writer
Margin notes

Sabon is the result of a 1960s commission fulfilled by the great typographer Jan Tschichold. The brief to create a modernised cut of Claude Garamond's sixteenth-century Humanist serif produced a typeface which isn't without its flaws, but at the time his Old Style interpretation answered the brief and provided typesetters with a quietly attractive and extremely flexible serif. The ever-faithful Gill Sans provides a sans serif peer for this classic Garamond revival.

On this page
Sabon
Gill Sans

BREATH

A sigh of relief

Gentle Murmur

Hushed undertones

SOFT

There are few display fonts that can rival the serenity of the SangBleu family, released by Swiss Typefaces in 2008. Two weights, Hairline and Light, come in two style variations with and without serifs, and both are exquisitely refined. Aging cousin Optima may look a little dated against this contemporary supermodel of a typeface but its tranquil beauty can't be denied, and Idlewild backs both up with a quite robustness that never shatters the placid silence.

On this page

SangBleu Sans
Optima
IDLEWILD

Client	Williams-Sonoma, Soaps and Lotions
Studio/Designer	Michael Osborne Design/Michael Osborne
Web	www.modsf.com
Principal typefaces	Bodoni, Lucia, Trade Gothic

Products designed to soothe as well as clean require a quietly reserved approach to the typography, and this upmarket and calm approach to the packaging achieves that without losing its shelf-presence.

Glossary

Aperture

The opening between the exterior and interior of a glyph.

Apex

The upper point at which the stems of a character meet to form a junction with an angle of less than ninety degrees, for example the top-most point of a capital 'A'.

Arc

A curved stroke that extends from a straight stem but does not form a bowl, for example, the top of a lowercase 'f' or the bottom of a lowercase 'j'.

Arm

A stroke that extends either horizontally from a vertical stroke or runs diagonally, for example, the top of an uppercase 'F' or the strokes of an uppercase 'X'.

Ascender

The part of a lowercase character that extends or ascends above the x-height of the other lowercase characters in a typeface, for example, the top part of the lowercase 'h' or 'd'.

Ball terminal

A circular termination at the end of an arm in characters such as lowercase 'a' or 'r'.

Beak

A sharp projection that usually appears at the end of the arc of a lowercase 'f', as well as in the characters 'c', 'j', 'r' and 'y'.

Bowl

The curved stroke enclosing the rounded or elliptical shape formed in characters such as 'B' or 'a'. Bowls can be closed or open, as seen in the lowercase 'b' of Fedra Serif.

Bracketed serif

A serif transitioning from the stem of a character in one unbroken curve, for example, the Transitional typeface Baskerville has bracketed serifs.

Cap-height

The height measured from the baseline to the top of uppercase letters in a font. This will not necessarily equal the height of the ascenders.

Colour

The tonal value or visual weight of a block of text, expressed as a greyscale. There are many factors that can influence typographic colour, including letterform style, stroke width, weight, size and leading.

Counter

The space formed within characters such as 'c' or 'g'. They can be open or closed and shouldn't be confused with bowls, which are in fact strokes.

Cross bar

The horizontal bar that connects two strokes in characters such as an uppercase 'A' or 'H'.

Cross stroke

The horizontal stroke that cuts across the stem of lowercase characters such as 'f' or 't'.

Crotch

The pointed space formed when an arm or an arc meets a stem, for example, in the inner top corner of an 'F'. Crotches can be either obtuse (more than ninety degrees) or acute (less than ninety degrees).

Descender

The part of a lowercase character that extends below the baseline of the other lowercase characters in a typeface, for example, the bottom portion of the lowercase 'p' or 'y'.

Double-storey

A lowercase 'a' with a closed bowl and a stem with a finial arm above, or a lowercase 'g' with a closed bowl and ear above a linked loop, for example, Adobe Jenson features a double-storey 'a' and 'g'.

Ear

The small projection that appears on lowercase characters such as 'g' in certain typefaces.

Expert characters

These have become increasingly outmoded since the advent of the OpenType format because all characters can now be incorporated into a single font for each weight, but there are still plenty of older format fonts in use today. Designed for Type 1 Postscript fonts, expert characters are non-standard letterforms extra to the standard character set, which may incorporate a swash or accent, or be an alternative form of a standard character.

Extenders

A common term used interchangeably for both ascenders and descenders.

Finial

A tapered, curved terminal at the end of a stroke, for example at the bottom of a 'C'. Swashes and ornamental flourishes are also commonly called finials.

Font

All the characters or glyphs for one style (or font file) within a font family. The terms 'font' and 'typeface' are often interchanged but there is a difference. This is best illustrated through the use of an example. Gotham is a typeface family; Gotham bold italic is a font.

Font family

All of the point sizes, weights and styles of one set of typefaces. A typical family consists of at least four styles; the most common are roman, italic, bold and bold italic. However, it's increasingly common to find superfamilies with ten or more weights ranging from thin to heavy.

Glyph

Each individual character in a font is a glyph; for example symbols and all the alternative forms for characters are individual glyphs.

Legibility

The measure of how easy it is to distinguish one letter of a typeface from another. The design of the typeface bears primary responsibility for the level of legibility, not the typographic styling of a layout.

Ligature

A single glyph composed of two characters paired together in certain combinations. Common examples are 'fi', 'fl' and 'Th', with the exact configuration dependent on the choice of typeface.

Loop

A closed counter that extends below the baseline and connects to a bowl by a link. A double-storey 'g' features a loop.

Lowercase

The uncapitalized characters of a typeface. The term derives from the fact that small letters were kept in the lower compartments of a type case when metal type was composed by hand. Historically, lowercase letters were known as minuscules.

OpenType

A font format developed jointly by Adobe and Microsoft. The primary advantage over previous formats is the ability to include up to 65,536 glyphs in a single font, plus advanced typographic features that allow the automatic substitution of alternative characters or glyphs in supporting applications such as InDesign or Illustrator. Font files are cross-platform and can be installed under both Mac OS and Windows.

Point

A unit of measurement that expresses font size. A point equals .0353 cm (0.0139 inches.

Point size

The height of the body of a typeface.

Readability

Readability isn't necessarily dependent on the legibility of the chosen typeface. It's primarily the responsibility of the designer. A highly legible font used poorly in a layout will not produce good readability.

Serif

In a serif typeface, the small stroke that completes the arms, stems, tails and descenders of individual characters.

Single-storey

A lowercase 'a' with a closed bowl and no finial arm above, or a lowercase 'g' with a closed bowl, stem and tail, for example, FS Dillon features a single-storey 'a' and 'g'.

Spur

The small projection that occurs at the terminals of some characters such as uppercase 'S' of Arnhem.

Stem

The main vertical strokes of a character, such as the upright strokes on either side of a capital 'H'.

Stress

The vertical, diagonal and occasionally horizontal emphasis suggested by a character's stroke. Horizontal stress is also referred to as reversed stress.

Stroke

The structural component of any character that is neither vertical nor horizontal. Stems are sometimes called vertical strokes, while crossbars can be called horizontal strokes.

Swash

An ornamental stroke extension used to add a decorative element to a standard character or glyph.

Tail

The descending stroke on characters such as the 'Q' or the bottom of the leg of an 'R'.

Terminal

The end of a stem or stroke.

Typeface

A set of characters, independent of individual point size, but with common classification characteristics, stroke widths, serif style and so on. The terms 'font' and 'typeface' are often interchanged, but there is a difference. This is best illustrated through the use of an example. Warnock is a typeface family; Warnock bold italic is a font.

Unbracketed serif

A serif that joins the stem of a character at a ninety-degree angle. Unbracketed serifs are a characteristic of Modern serif faces such as Bodoni.

Wedge serif

A serif that transitions from the stem of a character at an angled slope without curves. Linotype's distinctive Neue Swift is a fine example of a font with wedge serifs.

Weight

The thickness of a glyph's strokes. Type terminology uses the term 'weight' to describe individual fonts within a typeface family.

Width

Width can indicate whether a typeface has been either expanded or compressed when used as part of a font's name, for example 'condensed' or 'extended'. It can also be used as a general term to describe the average space occupied by a font's characters.

X-height

The height of a lowercase 'x'. The 'x' is used to define this measurement because it has no ascenders or descenders and no part of the character extends below the baseline.

The Type Foundries

Adobe: www.adobe.com

Alphabet Soup: michaeldoret.com

Elsner + Flake: www.fonts4ever.com

Emigre: www.emigre.com

Enschedé: www.teff.nl

Exljbris: www.exljbris.com

Fenotype: www.fenotype.com

Font Bureau: www.fontbureau.com

Font Shop International: www.fontshop.com

FontFont: www.fontfont.com

Fontsmith: www.fontsmith.com

Fort Foundry: fortfoundry.com

GarageFonts: www.garagefonts.com

GroupType: www.fonthaus.com

Hoefler & Co.: www.typography.com

Hoftype: www.hoftype.com

House Industries: www.houseind.com/fonts/

HVDFonts: www.hvdfonts.com

Lián Types: www.sproviero-type.com

Lineto: lineto.com

Linotype: www.linotype.com

Luxtypo: luxtypo.com

Mark Simonson: www.marksimonson.com/fonts

Monotype: www.monotype.com

MVB Fonts: www.mvbfonts.com

Our Type: ourtype.com

Parkinson Type Design: www.typedesign.com

Porchez Typofonderie: typofonderie.com

Positype: www.positype.com

Process Type Foundry: processtypefoundry.com

Rene Bieder: www.myfonts.com/foundry/Rene_Bieder/

S-Core: www.myfonts.com/foundry/S-Core/

Storm Type Foundry: www.stormtype.com

Suitcase Type: www.suitcasetype.com

Suomi: www.type.fi

Swiss Typefaces: www.swisstypefaces.com

T-26: www.t26.com

Terrestrial Design: www.myfonts.com/foundry/Terrestrial_Design/

Typejockeys: www.typejockeys.com

Type-O-Tones: www.type-o-tones.com

TypeTogether: www.type-together.com

TypeTrust: www.typetrust.com

Typotheque: www.typotheque.com

Underware: www.underware.nl

Urtd: www.urtd.net/fonts

(URW)++: www.urwpp.de

Village Constellation: vllg.com/constellation

Yellow Design Studio: www.yellowdesignstudio.com

Index

Acknowledgements

Typefaces are the stars in this title and without access to the two hundred or so typeface families featured we could never have made this book. I must therefore extended my thanks to all the type foundries and individual designers who provided fonts for us to use in Type Teams. Those people include Rene Bieder; Nicole Dotin; Zuzana Licko and Rudy VanderLans at Emigre; Samantha Grimsley-Franklin and the team at The Font Bureau, Inc; the team at FSI FontShop International GmbH; Jason Smith, Phil Garnham and the team at Fontsmith, Mattox Shuler at Fort Foundry; Ralph Smith at Garage Fonts; Melissa Marovich and the team at Hoefler & Co.; Hannes von Döhren at HVD Fonts; the team at Lineto; Ryan Martinson; Mark van Bronkhorst at MVB Fonts; Neil Summerour at Positype; Mark Simonson; František Štorm at Storm Type Foundry; Tomáš Brousil at Suitcase Type Foundry; Daniela at Swiss Typefaces; Veronika Burian and José Scaglione at TypeTogether; Ryan Martin at Yellow Design Studio. I would urge all readers to pay a visit to the individual websites listed on page 221 where at least one and in some cases several of the typefaces featured in our type teams can be sourced alongside many other exceptional typefaces which I would love to have included if I only had more room.

I'd also like to thank each of the designers who kindly provided examples of their work to demonstrate how type pairings can work in the 'real world' rather than as theoretical teams in the pages of this book. Please take some time to look over their online portfolios for more type team inspiration.

I'd like to thank Stephen Coles for his invaluable input to the project — as mentioned elsewhere in this book, choosing typefaces that work well together can be a very subjective pursuit so it was comforting to be able to draw on Stephen's extensive knowledge and experience.

Thanks to the team at Quid Publishing; James Evans and Nigel Browning for their continuing support and enthusiasm for books about typefaces, and Dee Costello for once again providing a constant level of editorial help and encouragement throughout the process.

There are sticking points during the writing of any book when one questions why on earth they agreed to do another. It's during those moments that the support of friends and family really count, and my wife Sarah has as ever been very accepting of the way I sometimes rant on endlessly about type. My thanks go to her, and to everyone else who helped to pick me up along the way.

First published in the United Kingdom in 2015 by Thames & Hudson Limited, 181A High Holborn, London WC1V 7QX

© 2015 Quid Publishing
Book design by Tony Seddon

Cover typefaces: Bodoni and Futura
The principal text throughout this book is set in Le Monde Livre and Benton Sans

British Library Cataloguing-in-Publication Data
A catalogue record for this book is available from the British Library

ISBN 978-0-500-29168-9

Printed and bound in China by 1010 Printing Group Ltd.

To find out about all our publications, please visit
www.thamesandhudson.com.
There you can subscribe to our e-newsletter, browse or download our current catalogue, and buy any titles that are in print.

Typeface and Foundry Required Copyright and Credit Information

Quadon designed by Rene Bieder / Amplitude, Tangier, Farnham, Giza, Heron Serif, Heron Sans, Poynter Gothic Text: The Font Bureau, Inc. / FF Yoga Sans, FF Unit Slab, FF Balance, FF Unit, FF Clifford & FF Scala: FontShop / FS Sinclair, FS Dillion, FS Emeric, FS Lola, FS Pimlico, FS Olivia and FS Clerkenwell: Fontsmith represents an international team working from a London studio, offering an extensive collection of typefaces alongside bespoke typefaces for global brands, design, and advertising agencies. / Industry: Mattox Shuler, Fort Foundry / Freight Micro Pro Family & Freight Text Pro Family: Garage Fonts / Acropolis, HTF Didot, Chronicle Display, Chronicle Text, Forza, Gotham, Gotham Condensed, Idlewild, Knockout, Leviathan, Mercury Display, Mercury Text, Requiem, Saracen, Sentinel, Topaz, Verlag, Vitesse, Whitney: Hoefler & Co. / Brandon Grotesque, Brandon Printed and Brandon Text designed by Hannes von Döhren, HVD Fonts, www.hvdfonts.com / Filosofia and Mrs Eaves designed by Zuzana Licko, 1996 / LL Akkurat designed by Laurenz Brunner, 2001-04. Published by Lineto.com, 2004 / LL Brown designed by Aurèle Sack, 2007-11. Published by Lineto.com, 2011 / MVB Solano Gothic and MVB Verdigris designed by Mark van Bronkhorst / Arnhem © Fred Smeijers, OurType.com / Lust Display, Lust Script, Lust Slim: Neil Summerour, type designer, Positype, http://positype.com, @positype Twitter & Instagram / Sangbleu: Swiss Typefaces, swisstypefaces.com, Ch. des Terrasses 4, 1820 Territet, Switzerland / Urban Grotesk: Tomáš Brousil, Suitcase Type Foundry / Beorcana designed by Carl Crossgrove, Terrestrial Design / Aniuk © Typejockeys 2014, www.typejockeys.com / Ingeborg © Typejockeys 2014, www.typejockeys.com / Fedra Sans and Fedra Serif: Typotheque / Abril and Abril Titling designed by Veronika Burian & José Scaglione, TypeTogether / Eskapade designed by Alisa Nowak, TypeTogether. / Pollen designed by Eduardo Berliner, TypeTogether / Eveleth and Gist: Ryan Martin, Yellow Design Studio